"Feel Ye"

"Feel Ye"

Poetic Reminiscence of an Octogenarian

SENTITO ET INTELLEGITO
"feel ye and thou shalt understand"

By

Robert Wood

W_PW
Wood Works Press

Dedication

To my all-encouraging family, Diana, Lise, Stephanie and son William and my dear wife Mary, and to all those who have shown me love, care, wisdom and who have stood by my side throughout my years without asking for anything in return.

To Doctor J. R. Broderson, DVM, PHD, who has given me, over the years, immeasurable encouragement, and an unbidden friendship, without which … who knows?

To Joe Mallonee, M.P.H., Deputy Commissioner of Public Health, State of Oklahoma, whose amity and phenomenal memory are truly valued.

To those who can reach into the depths of their sensitivities and be cognizant of the world around them.

About the Author

Navy veteran, Robert Wood, was born in Wyoming, lived in Midwest and all four quadrants of the U.S., Norway, Scotland, France, and has travelled widely, making do in five languages. Princeton, University of Minnesota, University of Edinburgh and the University of Oklahoma are his alma matters.

As a Doctor of Veterinary Medicine with post-doctoral degrees in Tropical Medicine and Epidemiology, and as a professor at Oklahoma State University and the University of Oklahoma, orchard grower, cattle feeder, angler, hiker, DIY'er, and a myriad of other interests, he has drawn upon his life to comment via poetry, urged on by family and friends. These poetically emotive works are just part of his pasticcio.

"It's all about communication"
Sculpture, Fonda Vela Hotel, Cloud Forest, Costa Rica
Photo: R. Wood

Acknowledgments

Thank you to Terri Wright for her assistance with producing the book, whose persistence, patience and tenacity, enabled the creation of a very gratifying publication. Without Terri, I probably would still be sitting at my desk pondering just how I was going to accomplish my endeavor. Her successes are reaped by her sensitive, detailed, and collaborative methodology.

also

Alpha Graphics in San Marcos, California, owner Gry Treiber, who was instrumental in assisting me over the initial glitchews, pitfalls, and choices in the provate printing of the first edition of Feel Ye, my deep gratitude go to him and his very competent staff.

Chapter Synopses

Chapter 1: **LOVE and NATURE**; Supreme Powers

Love of life, love of nature and personal individual love of family and others, reverberates throughout. The power of same is expressed with sensitivity by heartfelt phraseology, opening your inner reflective emotions. As the author states, "Feel to Understand".

Chapter 2: **RANCH and RANGE**; Poetic Musings

Lyric and narrative expressions of elation, reverence, and awe, take you to some of the author's life-experiences in the West. He grew up with ranching in his veins, chasing horses, cattle, women and whisky, not necessarily in that order with a good friend, Bill Valdez. From the old cowboy bronc-busters to today's 4WD, eco minded, tech savvy, ag-astute musters --- time marches on.

Chapter 3: **MY WORLD**; Emotivity of Bipolarity

A thought-provoking iteration of personal and philosophical revelations from a mind burdened with bipolarity, revealing not only a sometimes-caustic commentary on the exigencies of life, but yet, still life embracing. A randomized presentation as in a life of eighty-five years.

Chapter 4: **SHORTS and LIMERICKS**; Jocosity

Humor, ribaldry, acerbity, derision, and a few perturbations permeate these short works. Read and chuckle; a degree of jocularity is required

Contents

Foreword ······ xxiii

Introduction ··· xxv

Chapter I ············1

Love and Nature···1

Supreme Powers 1

Preamble ········2

To Love ··3

A Down Moment································ 4

Point Lobos Impressions·····················5

Grand Canyon ·······························6

Elusive One ································7

Inevitable ································8

Happy Birthday Old-Love ···················8

On Love································9

Enticement ····························· 11

Lakeside Evening ······················ 12

Please, No!································ 12

Seek Thee! ····························· 13

Bue Lights of Christmas ················ 14

As It Goes································ 14

Snowy Fragrance ······················ 15

Morning Reflections ··················· 16

Fervency ······························· 16

Declarative ·························17

Limited Love························ 18

Continuance ······················ 18

Good Morning!·····················20

Manatee ··························· 21

Nearness ·························· 21

Go Forth··························22

Love Received·····················22

Raindrops ·························24

Feelings (Haiku)··················25

Wishful ··························26

Epilogue ·························26

Grand Canyon Thoughts ···········26

The Mule ·························26

Completion ·······················27

Youth ···························27

The Hiker·························27

Trek·····························27

Us First··························28

Whispers ·························30

Love ····························· 31

Oceans of Love ···················· 31

Retrospection·····················32

Good Times ·······················33

Nature's Lullaby ································33

Our Love ······································34

Unfinished ···································35

Musical Interlude·························36

Distant Love·······························37

Fate ··38

Love, A Flower·····························38

Night ··40

Sunrise ·····································41

Unpredictability ·························42

Last Rose of Summer ··············42

Oceans of Emotions ·················43

Aegean Umbra Solis ················43

Autumnal Calling·······················44

Nap ···45

Blue Moon···································45

Silence·······································46

Prenuptial Doubts ····················47

One More Time ·························48

Súplica·······································48

No Limit ·····································50

And the Telephone Rings ···········50

Les Balons··································51

Fear···52

Morning Rise ⋯⋯⋯⋯⋯⋯⋯⋯⋯52

So Simple ⋯⋯⋯⋯⋯⋯⋯⋯⋯53

My Dream ⋯⋯⋯⋯⋯⋯⋯⋯⋯53

Classy Girl ⋯⋯⋯⋯⋯⋯⋯⋯⋯55

A Spider's Web ⋯⋯⋯⋯⋯⋯⋯⋯56

Snowy Fragrance ⋯⋯⋯⋯⋯⋯⋯57

Beauty ⋯⋯⋯⋯⋯⋯⋯⋯⋯⋯⋯57

Faith ⋯⋯⋯⋯⋯⋯⋯⋯⋯⋯⋯⋯58

PaPa Joe's ⋯⋯⋯⋯⋯⋯⋯⋯⋯⋯58

Can You Handle That ⋯⋯⋯⋯⋯59

Little Woman ⋯⋯⋯⋯⋯⋯⋯⋯60

If I were a snow flake ⋯⋯⋯⋯ 61

In Vain ⋯⋯⋯⋯⋯⋯⋯⋯⋯⋯⋯62

Celestially Speaking ⋯⋯⋯⋯⋯62

Just Italian ⋯⋯⋯⋯⋯⋯⋯⋯⋯63

Venture Out ⋯⋯⋯⋯⋯⋯⋯⋯64

Autumnal Calling ⋯⋯⋯⋯⋯⋯65

Supreme Power ⋯⋯⋯⋯⋯⋯⋯66

Love: A Falling Star ⋯⋯⋯⋯⋯66

Reasons ⋯⋯⋯⋯⋯⋯⋯⋯⋯⋯66

What Would I Do? ⋯⋯⋯⋯⋯ 67

Sanibel Shells ⋯⋯⋯⋯⋯⋯⋯⋯68

Under the Sun ⋯⋯⋯⋯⋯⋯⋯68

Importunity ⋯⋯⋯⋯⋯⋯⋯⋯69

Erotica ·· 70

Rekindle a Candle ······················· 70

Emotional Dynamism ··················· 71

Absence ··· 72

A Wave ·· 73

Contemplation ······························ 73

One-Under·· 76

Diminishing Return ······················ 77

I Miss You ···································· 78

The Question ······························· 78

Gray Titans ··································· 80

Away··· 80

My Love ·· 80

Soft as Velvet································ 81

I Guess, Kinda, Maybe·················· 82

Les Montagnes ······························ 83

Thoughts·· 84

Being a Zephyr······························ 84

Part 2 ... Family Endearments   85

Genealogically Speaking ·············· 85

Sister Dear···································· 87

The Man from Wyoming ·············· 89

Ah, The Memories! ······················ 92

On Occasion ·································· 93

JCB On Ninetieth ·······················97

Part 3 ... Emotions to Mother   97

Mother at 90, April 7, 2000 ··········97

Dissynchrony ····························· 100

While Waiting (2-05-03) ·············103

Until Death Do Us Part ·············108

A Lady's Grace ····························109

Part 4 ... To have and to hold   110

Just for You ···························· 110

I Remember ···························· 110

Back Then ···························· 112

I Used To Sing ························ 112

There Was A Time ·················· 113

Grief··································· 115

Widower's Lament······················ 115

Redefine Love ···················· 116

Part 5 ············118

Umbra Solis ···························· 118

Aperçu··································125

Chapter II ········127

Ranch and Range127

Poetic Musing 127

"V Rock" ·········127

Preamble ······128

The Procrastinator ··················129

Good Morning ·······················130

Call of The Mountains ·············· 131

Few Left··························· 132

Lightning Strikes···················133

Elusive One·······················134

Easy Drive ·······················134

Elegy to Curly ····················137

Night Stop ·······················139

Lochinvar ························140

I Guess, Kinda, Maybe·············· 141

Past Tense ·······················142

Pebbles ··························143

Morning ··························144

Eastern Law – Western Judge ········145

Room Service ·····················146

The Hike ·························148

Mountain Stream ··················149

Night Stillness ···················150

Ode to The Hunter ················ 151

Imagine··························152

Sage Advice ·····················153

Query···························156

Excursus·························158

Just a Thought ························158

CHAPTER III···· 163

My World········ 163

Emotivity of Bipolarity   163

Preamble ······163

My Intent ·······················165

Joy Killers ·····················165

Twenty-four Hours ···············166

Age-old Dilemma ················167

Duplicity ·······················167

Self-Analysis ···················168

Why? ···························168

Where Did It Go ·················169

Reasoning ······················169

Fate, Your Shadow···············170

How? ···························171

Preparation ····················172

At Eighty·······················172

Over ···························174

My Mary·························174

Passages·······················174

Coming Around ··················176

Evening·························177

Dream ··························178

Getting Old ···························178

Diestic Contemplation ···············180

Reflex ions ·························· 181

Hello Doctor! ·······················182

Darkest Time of Day··················183

Premonitions·························184

On Notice ···························184

Oh Wildwood··························185

Not Stopping? ·······················185

All Around Us ·······················186

You Just Don't Know··················187

Adjust ······························188

A Woman ···························189

What is Life?·························189

What we are Dealt····················189

Torn ································190

Time and Space ····················· 191

A Mind Not at Peace ·················192

Vis Vie ·····························192

Reflections II ·······················193

Dilemma? ···························194

Twilight ····························195

Temptation ··························196

Hell No!!!···························196

Old Things ···197

The Littered Trail ····························197

Hello Again ·······································198

Dejection··199

Inner self ··200

Think for yourself ····························200

Feel Every Dream ······························201

June 2008 ··202

It Ain't So Bad Being Man ···········203

On Aging··204

The Years Pass On ·························204

Plight··205

Remember ···206

Your Heart··206

Dolts ··206

Where to From Here ·····················207

Frustrated Horticulturist ··············208

Why, One Day···································209

Disgust ···209

What's Better? ·································210

Trail to Nowhere ····························211

Divisional Man ·································211

The Far Side of Sanity···················212

Life's a Limerick·····························213

Self-snuff ················· 215

Introversion ·············· 215

About A Poet ··············· 216

Verdens Ende ·············· 217

Le Bouton ················· 218

Look Thee Not ············· 219

Dérèglement ··············· 220

Musings on Getting Old ······ 220

Slow Down ················· 221

Musings on Aging ··········· 222

Act as You Feel ············ 223

A Bipolar's Supplication ······ 224

Descry Love ··············· 224

Think Good Times ·········· 225

Encroaching Horizons ······· 225

Women ··················· 226

Chicken Liver ·············· 227

Theory of Creativity ········· 228

Strength ·················· 229

Perturbed ················· 229

Don't Leave a Hot Woman ····· 230

Double Standard ··········· 230

Generational Changes ······· 231

Why, What? ··············· 232

Good-Bye Creativity ···················· 233

The Darker Side of Light ·············· 233

Bipolarity ···························· 235

What path? ··························· 235

Supreme Power ······················ 236

And There Goes The Sun ············· 236

All Rise ···························· 237

Laryngitis Rx ······················· 238

Numbers 11/12/13 ················· 239

Stuff: ····························· 239

Why is the Why? ···················· 240

Ego and The Creative Spirit ··········· 241

A Stranger in My Mind ··············· 242

Just Please ······················· 242

The Creative Mind ·················· 243

Dichotomy ························· 244

Speak Up ·························· 244

Haunts ·························· 244

Conversation with Self ·············· 246

Dark Hole ······················· 248

Self-justification ·················· 249

Stigma ··························· 250

State of Self (age 85) ··············· 250

Sunset Thoughts ·················· 252

Disquietude ·························· 253

Why Bother ························· 254

Talking To: ························· 255

Carpe Diem ························· 256

Willingness ························· 257

My Life ······························ 257

Mindfulness ························ 258

Tired ································· 259

February 13th ····················· 259

Darkness ·························· 261

One More Time ················· 261

Chapter IV ······**263**

SHORTS and LIMERICKS   263

Preamble ····· 263

Heritage ························ 263

Quest ···························· 263

Genesis ························· 264

Priorities ······················· 264

Guidance ····················· 264

Embarrassment ··············· 265

Effort ···························· 265

Arrogance ····················· 265

Bragging ······················· 265

Society ························· 266

Friends In Need ························ 266

Climbers ································· 266

Evil Doer ······························· 266

"Kiss" (Keep it simple, stupid) ······ 267

Table Manners ························· 267

Self-Control ··························· 267

Tread Lightly ························· 267

Goals ································· 268

Preoccupation ······················· 268

Convictions ························· 268

The Snottier Side ·················· 268

Self-assurance ····················· 269

Money Hole ······················· 269

Marital Morality ·················· 269

Inferiority ······················· 270

Addle Headed ····················· 270

People ··························· 270

Political Animosities ·············· 270

Family ··························· 271

Overly Analytical ················ 271

Religiosity ····················· 271

Let-down ······················ 272

Word Play ···················· 272

Cooking ······················ 272

Clothing ································· 273

Women ································ 273

Mystery ······························ 273

Mystique ····························· 273

Red Neck Socialite ················· 274

Nosey Ones ·························· 274

Less is More ························· 274

Few Words ··························· 275

Stats ································· 275

Not Relevant ························ 275

More Stats ·························· 275

More Stats 2 ························ 276

MD Escapism ························ 276

Ants ································· 276

Auto Arrogance ····················· 276

Sing a Song ························· 277

Fads ································· 277

Commerce ··························· 277

Eco 101 ····························· 278

Eco 102 ····························· 278

Living Rationale ····················· 278

Depression ·························· 278

America ····························· 279

Maturity ····························· 279

Your Cheek ·································· 279

Your Children ·························· 279

Parental Wrong? ···················· 280

Speak Your Piece ·················· 280

The Change ···························· 280

Frustration ···························· 281

You to Me ······························ 281

Arrogance ······························ 281

Numbers Together ·················· 281

Observe ································ 282

Sicily ·································· 282

Etherion ································ 282

Mars ···································· 282

Poetic Regimen ···················· 283

Domesticity ·························· 283

Unhappy Patient ···················· 283

Psychiatrist ························ 283

My Lady ································ 284

Sagacity ······························ 284

Vanity ·································· 284

Cooking ································ 284

Sewing ·································· 285

Polishing Shoes ···················· 285

Ironing ································ 285

Drivers ···················· 285

Lack of Curiosity ·············· 286

Complainers ················· 286

Determination ··············· 286

Why ····················· 286

Deception ·················· 287

Gentleman's ················· 287

A Woman ··················· 287

Intellect ··················· 287

Talk Talk ·················· 288

Maiden's Cry ················ 288

Mysterious One ·············· 288

Lady in Waiting ············· 288

To Bed ···················· 289

Control ··················· 289

Maternal Flaw ·············· 289

Windwalker ················· 289

Me, Myself and I ············· 290

Too Late ·················· 290

Boats ···················· 290

The Party ·················· 291

Barista Louisa ·············· 291

Seventies ·················· 292

Patriotic Old Driller············ 292

More Stats ································ 293

Gobble-Gobble ······················· 293

Ace Hardware························· 294

Rocky Springtime ···················· 294

Weatherman·························· 294

Frustration Avoidance················· 294

Boar's Butt ························· 295

Over-rated ························· 295

Carmel····························· 295

Job-site flirtation ··················· 296

Senorita Superiority ················· 296

Admonishment······················· 296

Sergeant Cook ······················ 296

Expectancy ························· 297

A Woman ·························· 297

The Beckoning Way ················· 298

Color Your World ·················· 298

I Am ····························· 298

The Therapist ····················· 299

BPPV ····························· 299

Booze and Wine ··················· 299

Bill Fish ························· 299

Life ····························· 300

Lazy ····························· 300

Autumn ··· 300

Whispers ·· 300

Expectations ·· 301

Materialism ·· 301

Hurry ··· 301

Morality ··· 302

Epicurean ·· 302

In Flagranti ··· 302

Change ··· 303

Quit Dreamin' ······································ 303

Last Dish ··· 303

Negativity ·· 303

Post Prandial "Prime Ten" ················· 304

Long Gone Doggie Blues ················· 304

Remodel Blues ····································· 305

Time & Rhyme ····································· 306

Foreword

"Poetry is oft times a window to the soul, cloudy or clear as is the want of the poet." Helen Vendler, in the *Paris Review*, remarked about the importance of poetry: "Lyric and verse can be faithful and lifelong companions, personal resources, and aids in times of anxiety and distress." *

Appearing in an article in the Princeton Alumni Weekly, June 7th, 2006 by Dan-el Padilla Peralta.

"If I create from the heart, nearly everything works; if from the head, almost nothing."   *Chagall*

"……. your words are so beautiful, and I'm sitting here weeping after reading it. I hope to continue being teachable and learn how to love like you do. The state of your heart is second to none.
Written by an unbiased daughter, 2009

Introduction

Poetry is the cognitive evolvement of one's feelings and emotions in a manner that is most reflective of sensitivities. It can be light and loose, classical and staid, whimsical or narrational or a plethora of combinations. Consider the probability of a phrase occurring from a lexicon of more than one million words in the English language, and you have an almost infinite number of verbal expressions open to the poet. That is an awesome pallet!

The poet is an artist with boundaries so wide that they are literally unimaginable and perhaps immeasurable to an extent; and therein lays his safety. His method of expression can certainly be scrutinized and criticized, but seldom can what he has to say be censored, if there is freedom of thought and speech. If the main thrust of his attempted conveyance is to elucidate in some fashion and not to aspire to achieve an academic level of acceptance as a poet per se, then he will be successful.

A poet paints his thoughts with words; and the sometimes not so subtle juxtaposition of one word against the other, one phrase against the other or one subject against another. His palette consists of not only the unbelievably rich English language, but the ability to enhance what he is thinking by the use of words from other languages that have been generally accepted by the literate public, i.e. merci. Furthermore, if need be, he can go beyond English propriety and embellish an already existing word to suit his needs as long as there is clarity of meaning; that can be referred to as poetic license – a neologism.

Let the creators of poetry have the pleasure of attempting verbal conveyance in whatever fashion suits them. Butterflies fly in a predictably erratic pattern. Enjoy flights of fancy in a similar way. If a thought is elusive, close the eyes. Just as there is method acting, there is method writing – get inside what you are trying to write about. Immerse yourself so completely that you cry at a moment of hurt, you chuckle at a moment of mirth. If you write about anger, your blood pressure should go up. If you write about the desert, your body temperature should go up, literally, and conversely, it should go down if you write about the artic. Live what you are trying to put on paper.

My pasticcio are expressions of intense happiness, joy, humor, seething frustrations, commentary, melancholia, philosophical bromides, directives, invectives, whimsicality, resentment and resignation. In other words: life. They may refer to places I've been, situations that I have had to deal with, toasts, boasts and self-denigrations. I challenge others to interpret my verbal palette. Let them absorb my ideas and find out from whence they came.

Relax and enjoy
Verses transitional,
And a pleasant departure
From Shakespearean traditional.

Some without metrics;
Narrational and chimerical,
Prophetic and poetic,
And usually lyrical.

Written to all ages
Without specific gender,
To entertain and amuse,
Some more rough than tender

Chapter I

Love and Nature
Supreme Powers

"feel ye and thou shall understand"

Nature begets Love begets Nature

Inside Passage, Canada; Photo: R. Wood

Preamble

Nature and love, from two different Latin roots, *natura* and *libet*, amongst others, though different, are irrevocably juxtaposed to each other. As is stated, "nature begets love begets nature". Is not the phenomena of the physical world collectively conducive to love? And is not love conducive to taking care of and nurturing, exactly what nature needs.

The following poems from each sphere demonstrate in part what the author feels about each one, intertwined or separately. Immerse yourself as reading, be there, think it, imagine it --- and enjoy.

To Love

To love is to learn,
To awaken to another's senses,
To feel pain when you have none,
Excruciating, though not yours,
A vain attempt to help carry the load
Of heartache that may rip at your treasure.

To love is to forget,
Forget the meaningless trivia
That can clog the veins of tomorrow,
That plaque of erosive emotion,
That senseless corrosive entanglement
That burdens what should be free.

To love is to embrace dual ideologies
Waiting to take flight,
Waiting to creatively soar.
Dualism is the key, not singularity,
A cohesive bond moving through life,
Absorbing, hearing, awakening.

To love is to realize that night is day.
There is no real sleep, only rest
Between twenty-four hours of sensing.
To realize that you are one,
Moving, swaying, pulsing to another beat
Not yours, but an ethereal genesis.

To love is to magnify your perception,
To see more, hear more, feel more,
To feel touch when not there,
To heighten the attraction,
To reach further,
When a grasp may be tenuous.

To love is not just one plus one,
But the combination of two sets of five senses
Raised to the heightened power,
Exploding in organized chaos,
With no control, or care.
Learn! Don't let it go.

A Down Moment

The lights are out
The passion is gone.
The heart is deaf
To the siren's song.

The days drone on
In unending drab
To reveal a relationship
That now has gone bad.

The release isn't clear,
But there's one thing for sure
If sanity is to prevail,
There has got to be a cure.

Is there ever an age
When you're really too old
To care what matters
Or to stop being bold?

I wish it would happen
'Cause I am really too tired
To chase another,
And in a union get mired.

Is there any use in trying
To search and find one,
To delude yourself
Till the flirting's done.

And awaken once more
To realize the mistake,
The heart you have broken
Cause of some stupid mistake.

Don't make trash
Of another's sensitivity,
Because one more time
You've followed your proclivity.

Point Lobos Impressions
Carmel, California

When it's breeding time in the pacific,
The bull seals get quite specific.
The cows think it's all terrific,
The object is to be prolific.

The seals have a tale to spiel,
The otters an urchin to peal,
The fish have a fervent wish,
Not be served as a chafing dish.

No way to gage
The tidepool's age,
Nor the beauty and fragrance
Of the blue-gray sage.

The Monterey Pine
Is a tree so fine
For the Osprey to rest,
And raise the best.

Is the Fidler a piddler
Or a crab to respect?
Is nature magnificent
On which to reflect?

Grand Canyon

I dreamed about the Grand Canyon,
I prepared for what I had to do.
I developed an attitude
For courage to execute the total plan through.

What plan, say I?
A monumental endeavor
For one with seventy-six years?
A traverse of the Canyon ... clever!

From sunrise to sunset,
Rim to Rim in just one sun,
From the wee hours of the morn,
To the fading light when the day is done.

I wanted to see Her,
I wanted to be near Her,
I wanted to be in the Canyon,
And hear Her stir.

And now I have viewed Her glory,
I have felt Her sinew and more.
She has talked to me in a whisper
And I have heard Her roar.

I have smelled the nuances
In the day's progression, between hot and cold.
I've tasted the morsels from nature's bountiful plate.
Yes! The Canyon is in my soul.

So, listen my fellow seniors!
Hear something you can't refute!
Pace yourselves!
Prepare, get an Attitude for the Courage to Execute.

And all you senior wana-be's,
Don't languish in the interlude,
Because the puffing you hear behind you,
Just may be a SENIOR with an ATTITUDE

Elusive One

What timid shadow is that,
stirring on the gravely interface
of sublimity and reality?
That elongate dream of detached amusement,
That flash of color
racing between sun and rock,
That soft apparition
floating from cloud to cloud?

What chance to glimpse
God's perfect shape,
The plexus of geometric form,
Yet independent attitude
mirror-imaging the soul,
The nidus of serendipitous dream.
Yours is the heaven that exists
In the cool rush of the mountain stream.

Inevitable

Flickering candle flame,
How you illuminate the shadows.
Glimpsing pathways to future fantasies,
Warming the moment.

Then that cold breeze.
Why are you dying?
Your flame shrinks
In the face of ardor.

Coolness prevails.
The light is dimmer.
The final snuff.
Is it really out?

The warmth lingers.
The last curl of dream-laden smoke,
And it disappears.
And then the cold wick.

An alive beacon
Gone dead over time.
Inanimate now.
A past sublime.

Happy Birthday Old-Love

Take the test of years gone by!
Can you think back to moments when
Your mind went giddy with anticipation,
Now that you are three score and ten?

Years fleet by in the twinkle of an eye.
So, Dear Lady, our horizons focus more clearly.
Clouded visions only sharpen with time,
Our memories will serve us more dearly.

If you can remember like I can remember,
Then passion has no definition.
If, without guilt, you have felt what I have felt,
Then there's no need for an act of contrition.

If every star in the sky makes you ponder why
Our lives have taken this turning;
And every moon-lit night is a re-lived moment,
Then heaven's glow just elucidates our emotional yearning.

What you can grasp, yet cannot be touched,
If your feelings hold true, never to stray,
A perception that is as evasive as a summer zephyr,
Then there is a love that's all inclusive …
and one that's here to stay.

May your life be filled with unbounded love
and your aspirations…know no limits!

On Love

True love is but a fleeting glimpse of the hereafter
Heralded, marginally touchable,
Incredibly fragile when mishandled,
And as durable as bedrock … impenetrable.

Love is as different from man
Than woman and man themselves.
Rough maybe, but desperately trying to be soft.
Caring, sensitive, inept perhaps … expressing élan.

9

Man's love can be needy, greedy, speedy
Fraught with passion, yet incomplete.
Bolstered by macho, the urge to protect;
The urgency, the hunger ... the inability to repeat.

The ensuing frustration of those unsated,
Resting heavily on the sensitive mind.
What bond can be established
To capture, to prove one's mettle? ... the elusive find.

The emptiness, the feeling of defeat,
Of inability to express your heart
So that the message conveyed
Screams ... until death do us part.

Why were we constructed inside and out
With such deficiencies, unable to express
Our inner desires, our longings, our natural mandates
To convince irrevocably ... our words to caress?

Maybe these liabilities are apparent to just us
And our calling gets through
To a receptive heart
That has the ability to recognize ... that which is true.

And what of woman whose timorous affections
Are a mockery of the strength, vitality, of a love that is deep?
Hidden from man until summoned up by an inner power
That was engendered when "x,x" chromosomes prevailed ... in a
previous sleep.

No man can begin to understand the birthing pain and joy;
Nor can he fathom the embryogenic unconditional love,
That unwavering, ocean floor of feeling
That is as steady as its antitheses are not ... the waves above.

Yet those waves can rock the loved one, or rage and storm
With arms that reach out to continually embrace
The most intimate aspects of what it envelopes;
And nurture and grow its treasure ... and never show its face.

If per chance that love escapes from its maternal charge
To love again in another dimension,
The love received, not compromised but true,
Is mind staggering ... beyond comprehension.

How wonderful it must be to know intuitively
That this purity exists as an undelivered gem,
A controllable emotion
To be given only to whomever ... where and when.

And in so doing raise the horizons to a new level
For the recipient and the one who gives,
But only if reciprocated in an acceptable fashion;
Recognizable and felt ...   for as long as one lives.

Oh, how fortunate for I feel the union complete.
Somehow able to surmount the barrier of intelligibility
And through touch, word and deed,
Meld a bonding of body and soul ... a total tranquility.
Man, and woman's love may not be the same,
But between you and me, dearest one,
We have everything to gain.

Enticement

A zephyr's caress, the shadow of a butterfly wing,
Rainbows undress her soul, to vulnerability ...
A tenderness there to find the character beneath,
Resiliency, love, stalwart ... gifts to bequeath.

Lakeside Evening

There's a crescent moon barely holding water.
The blue is darkening into dusk.
I look, see the last-glimmering of the day on the water,
A few ripples from playful otters.

Jagged peaks, a chiaroscuro with the twilight.
The day is all but done,
Except for where it arises on another horizon,
Awaiting rebirth of the sun.

Here I say goodbye to the day I have seen,
Goodbye to the sights of the diurnal beings;
Goodbye to the creatures of the light
And Hello! – to the creatures of the night.

Why a melancholy air?
Why is there the burden of trepidation?
Perhaps the fear for a hidden mistake,
That in the morning I should not wake.

But creation turns as it always has
And what goes around, comes around again.
Tenuously, the living evolve
And round and round the world revolves.

Please, No!

If you're feeling lonely,
If you're feeling blue,
I ask you sweet Darling,
Just what I mean to you.

Were not the love words spoken
Meaningful at all?
Were not the moments shared,
Supposed to soften any fall?

Did not I let you know
Just what you mean to me?
Where did I fail, ...
My love for you to see?

Is the twilight in your heart
Reflected in your eyes?
Do not my tears of anguish
Catch you by surprise?

Did I stumble as a man?
Did not my feelings show?
Lord, please tell me why,
Before you decide to go.

Seek Thee!

What long lost glimmer of faded-love,
Lurks beneath social amity?
What, that true feelings should be so suppressed,
Not nourished to flourish again
Before twilight dims all!

Norms negate all but adventurists
To speak out seeking truth.
But the complacent: lost to all,
All wonders of allure in amour.
An acceptance of emotional mediocrity!

To those, not to seek again,
Those whose contentment belie reality,
Those destined for stultification
From uplifting virtues
Of freedom from incarceration.
                    Steep in your own quagmire!

Bue Lights of Christmas

The blue lights of Christmas,
Beacons in the night
To the heart and its tremulous tendrils;
Everything is alright.

Not just anywhere,
But of such magnitude,
That there could be no doubt,
That my love has no latitude,

But is singularly directed
To the one I love;
Greater than all the blue lights,
Or all the stars above.

The blue lights may wink off
To a season gone by,
But never my emotions.
Never can they die!

As It Goes

May a snow flake land upon your nose.
May Jack Frost tickle your toes.
The temperature is in the lows.
Feel the cold north wind as she blows.

Dead leaves lie in rows.
To the south, have gone the crows.
Deer are seen though, bucks and does.
Packages are covered with bows.
Good cheer flows.
Ice may cover the rose,
But the gardeners have put away their hoes.
In Springtime what do you suppose?
There are no more wintry woes.

If there's more, who knows?

Snowy Fragrance

A snowy fragrance is ore the land
And all about us, clean.
Nature's housework is now done,
And all the land's serene.

The twigs and trunks are painted white,
The boughs bend low with cotton.
The earth, asleep under undulating folds,
Nothing has been forgotten.

As I look out upon this harmony,
I cannot help but ponder
What really wraps around us;
And in what direction will life wander.

Heaven is here …
But for us to ask.
The Lord has applied his art;
And in its beauty, we doth bask.

15

Morning Reflections

Your early morning shadow
Like sunrise on the plain.
The softness of your shoulder,
A golden hue of waving grain.

The light upon your skin,
A chiaroscuro of tenderness.
Your cheek, a rose's petal,
A fragrance's sweet caress.

Your sleeping face
To wakefulness arrives.
Eyes of devotion,
Your parted lips to join our lives.

Your extended arms, your smile,
All this, a new day to start.
It's more than I can fathom,
A love to never part.

Fervency

The world turns
And for some it stops.
That's inevitable ...
Like falling rain drops.

But that's not the point.
Just let the last glimpse be
Of flowers and blue sky
And white foam upon the sea.

I long for peace and quiet,
And cherish good clean air;
The lullaby of nature,
Visual freedom to spare.

Let the sun rise
And your sun set
On love not lost.
And to none ... in debt!

Declarative

Oh, Dear Love you're my wild flower,
Growing ore the lea.
You're a jasmine of such sweet fragrance,
That soon you'll be the melting of me.

You're there in the heather
That blooms lushly on the meadow,
Showing lovely hues amongst the green.
I hear you in the wren's sweet love song,
Hoping for a union, oh so keen.

You're with me when there is a duskiness on the hillside
And the day draws to a close.
You're as tender as the blue fading to a soft gray,
While the nighttime falls on the primrose.

My Love, there will be a full moon arising,
Illuminating all for me to see.
And I see you in my life forever,
Sweet Mary, lovely Mary, thank you for marrying me.

Limited Love

Love, what a nebulous, tenuous word!
Hardly a term without borders.
Exclusivity prays on the mind -
Undetermined duration upon whim.

Such is each day enfolding life.
Such is our amorous fate.
"Agape", God's love?
Don't hold your breath!

Continuance
Elk Birth

Motionless on the meadow,
She stands there with wonderment and expectation,
No restlessness, just waiting.
A course, mandating relaxation.

Not feeding, the hunger is wane,
Just looking, little movement, except internal.
Rest, saving energy.
Growing feelings, maternal.

A different movement now,
The call for genetic continuation.
The muscles contract,
The process of dilation.

The forefeet first,
Then the head.
The miracle of nature
And the calf lies on the grassy bed.

Mother elk now turns
And with caressing tongue,
Stimulates response
In the very young.

Clean and invigorated,
The infant struggles to its feet;
Wobbly, unsure, insecure,
Cool air, brightness, a new world to meet.

Attentively, the mother looks around,
Alert, lest something interfere.
She nudges, seeking more movement,
Intent on teaching one so dear.

A few steps this way
And then a slight stagger that,
Then a meandering away,
And quick movement back.

Oh, the joy to witness this new beginning.
Through binoculars we watch with awe,
Life's new evolvement,
With nary a flaw.

They go together,
Crossing the meadow green.
She hops the running rivulet,
And begs her calf to cross the stream.

With an effort Herculean,
The little fellow makes it across;
And literally, claws its way up the bank,
Collapsing in slumber, for energy lost.

She's wise and moves off a way.
Let her infant sleep!
Its dusk now and our eyes grow dim.
She'll move her young into the forest deep.

Good Morning!

Have you ever seen the rising sun through a drop of rain in the
morning light,
The awakening of the dawn from the previous night?

Have you watched as the mountains take shape, a mold coming into
view,
Or watched the gentle movement of the spider's web all covered with
silvery dew?

Have you heard the early heralding twitter, the stories that are told
By the restless young, their parents, the feathered, young and old?

Have you seen an ant, one side in light, the other in shade
As he ascends a wavering stem, an aphid for a meal to be made?

Have you watched a mountain stream come to life,
The critters and creatures, twigs and things, singing like a distant fife.

Have you realized that the tumbling never stops, it always caries on,
Breathing a message to a darkness gone?

Have you listened to the utter complete silence of an early morn,
The newness and sweetness of a day reborn?

Have you felt the gentle touch of the breeze upon your face
And realized that this is God's holy place?

Manatee

Who are you, oh creature of the glade,
With baleful eyes and a soul so deep?
Your languid movements propel you silently
With purpose, though seemingly asleep.

You seek the green from salty shallows
And drink from fresh water where found.
You frolic together in slow motion,
Yet often singular, alone, no sound.

'Sea Cow', elephant and hyrax relative,
Bewhiskered, grasping proboscis, behemoth,
What can you tell us of your ways,
You lovable, gentle, aquatic mammoth?

I've seen your bow wake in still waters,
I've seen you close – I've seen you afar.
Yet most mysterious one,
I long to know just who you are!

Nearness

Would not that love be ne'er requited,
Though both feel openly invited.
Now, best they swoon in memory only,
To temper lives too lonely,
For together, they'd get too excited!

True, they'd be rapturously delighted,
To have their loves reignited;
She the queen
And he to preen.
Then, they'd be properly united.

21

Go Forth
On the departure of a loved-one.

Upon what paths dare we tread?
Upon what presumption
Do we deign to equalize ourselves
To the life of such a lady?

What courage did she impart
For us to continue,
Beneath a shadow so large?
Proof of her work, is for us to start.

Go forth with trepidation,
But let not our fears succeed
In unraveling her labors of love,
For in her image we must excel in deed.

Our memories are our guidance
To fields unknown;
Heralded by spring,
With flowers sewn.

Love Received

A pathway in the mountain,
A blue violet,
And you.

Green soft ferns,
A babbling brook,
And you.

Timid blue butterflies,
Utter trust,
And you.

Endless blue sky,
A gray cloud,
And you.

Rainbow's hues,
The softness of heaven,
And you.

Is there a more profound
Statement of love,
Than that which I feel?

I think no man
Should want for greater richness,
Than his love, as I have mine.

Your love emanates
From your soul's depth,
From that core of loveliness.

And I can only try
To reciprocate in return,
A mere particle of love received.

Dreams can come true,
Don't dismay.
A love can be found,
In a very special way.

Raindrops

Cascading down to cleanse your mind,
Rushing, drifting to their own cadence,
Chattering or clamoring to their rhyme.

Wetting, or whetting your appetite
To enjoy their singular direction;
Numbers preempting selection.

The washing of the soul,
The rejuvenation of your being;
Each drop, growth you're seeing.

Rushing pell-mell to their destiny,
Each a pure jewel;
Potential happiness – not cruel.

Like life, every moment a gem
To treasure for its value;
A memory just for you.

And what of the memory?
What of the rain drop?
These things don't just stop.

They're meant to stimulate!
They mutate, rotate, compensate,
Procreate, exacerbate, and placate!

Like mountains and plains,
Pandora 's Box of diamonds and dimes,
Only discernable after time.

Feelings (Haiku)
(syllables, 5-7-5)

Legitimacy
Society creating
Strength and coherence

Mummifying cold
Suppressing cacophony
Musicality

Leaves cascading down
Season's past, peeling away
Rejuvenation

Nature – natural
A gift of tranquility
Mandates observance

Irrepressible
Love, hopelessly entangled
Irresistible

Walk in the desert
Not just for conversation
Listen to the quiet

True agape love
Irrevocability
Bliss - eternity

Wishful

I want to imprint myself
Indelibly on your mind.
I want you to think of me, as thine -
During your wakeful hours.

I want your dreams, most glorious.
I want all I can have and then some.
I want me to be a part of you
Forever more.

Epilogue

Fantasy, lived on, consumed by.
Reality, what meets the eye!
Dreams are but embellishments
On sought after sentiments.

Grand Canyon Thoughts
On completion of an R2R, 24-hour traverse – age 76

The Mule

The slope is steep
But the pace you keep.
For O_2, there is deprivation
At an ever-increasing elevation.
Don't slow to a creep!

An odor you begin to smell,
But from where you cannot tell.
Then it hits you in the face,
And you have to slow your pace.
Fourteen mules ahead, have just let go.

Ah! The amalgamation of grain and grass.
Doesn't Nature have any class?
It is all part of the climb.
That's what makes it so sublime.
God made that lovely ass.

Completion

It's not just the job you've done,
Or your perception for what's fun;
It's the fact that you've persisted,
While others have resisted.
You've achieved what you had begun.

Youth

The resiliency of youth
I find intolerable and uncouth.
So, suffice it to say,
They should get out of my way;
That's my proclamation, forsooth!

The Hiker

Idiocy prevails
Along the dusty trails.
From one point to another,
With friend or brother,
Solely, to tell the tale.

Trek

The ultimate trek you say,
Down to the bottom where you can't stay!
Then climb to the top,
Before you can stop,
All in a given day?

But wait, there's more,
You're incredibly sore.
Your body's wracked with pain,
For an infinitesimal gain;
Except for some cocktail lore.

Ah! The question is why
We reach for the sky.
We laugh and we groan,
Urged on by testosterone,
Until the day we die.

So be it, that's me!
Suits me to a "T".
I am who I am
That's what makes me a ram.
Just part of life, you see.

******

Us First

People come
And People go,
And people
Fall in love you know.

But lest we make others
Entirely nauseous,
Best we be,
A wee bit cautious.

Some wish us well,
Some don't care.
Some wish the hell
We'd get out of their hair.

Jealousy abounds,
And that's too bad;
Its our exultation
That makes them sad.

I won't change
And I hope you won't either.
I'll not stop,
Not even for a breather.

I'll show my affection
To you my dear.
That you can count on,
Have no fear.

And you to me,
Had better not stop,
Or so help me God;
My heart will pop.

You show me the utmost
Pleasure and love,
To stop that now
Will bring wrath from above.

So, let's carry on
The way we were.
Only the lucky,
Can hear us purr.

Whispers
Trailside realization - devotion

Silence whispers melodies.
Stop! Can't you hear?
There! There it is again,
Music! But where?

Melodious, gentle, caressing
The fantasies of your mind.
Rocking you softly, gently.
An answer to a prayer?

But your mind is dubious.
Flee! You have to.
Why? Who said?
On some tablet, some law

Surmised but not read?
I think not, love is rare.
An intangible happening,
You have to care.

Open the portals!
Let it in!
Let the silence tell all!
Let your heart and mind act in concert!

Let it escalate!
Let your resistance fall!
Listen! Whisperings!
"To yourself, be kind!"

Let the rainbows of your heart
Give guidance to the morrow.
Let the heavens light a spark,
An ember light your way.

 Let it build a burgeoning love,
So your days are utter bliss.
Let the sunset of today
Be the sunrise to eternity.

"Come, rise with me in crescendo,
Live with me in passion.
Let a thousand angels brush your face,
As you sleep with me in satisfaction."

Love

What is love?
The joyous enrapture of life
And very thing that's in it?
Or a dispassionate relationship between
Two ought-to-be's,
Brought together through
Propinquity?
A mutually tolerant coexistence?

Oceans of Love

Love's sweet waves,
Power surges
of emotional undulations.
Rocking gently,
The voices speak.

All sounds,
All glorious,
Caressing the inner self.
Music that can't be forgotten
Echoes in the mind,
Hearts that intertwine.

Tides of sadness, happiness,
Unrevealing by nature.
Full circles of serenity and pain,
Only to be forgotten
And remembered again,
And coveted,
And cherished.

The swelling heart,
The need for release.
All part of Neptunian magnitude,
Persistent in quietude.

Retrospection

From the barren plain of desultory function
To the spring of vibrant vitality!
Your pulse, my life,
Desiccates spiritless notions.

Aimless fantasia to meaningless quotients,
A life of senseless motions.
A flee from subjection ...
To love's consecration.

Delivered at last, vacuous existence,
Free of the past, lack of insistence.
Allowance of full devotion,
To swim in heavenly bliss.

Serene rhythmicity,
From abyss to apogee and beyond.
Your heart, my universe, my eternal energizer.
Bonded, undivided union, none wiser.

Children of God, hand in hand.
The preordained path,
Passaged though time.
Two souls in apposition.

Good Times

Think about the good things, not the bad.
Think about the happy moments, not the sad.
Think about the moments of utter bliss
that I know you and I had
And think about the wonderful times that we will miss ...
When we allow ourselves to reminisce?

Nature's Lullaby

Have you ever stopped to listen
To the myriad of languages, nature speaks;
From the thunderous moaning of frozen lakes,
To the whimsical laughter of riffles in a creek?

The gaggle of geese overhead on a mission,
Or the roar of a tumultuous storm,
To the leaf-drop preparation,
To a coming white season, yet unborn.

She speaks, night and day long.
The barely audible whoosh of the hunting owl,
The crack of an ancient descending to the ground,
Or the eerie cry of a lone wolf on the prowl.

Are you aware that an opening spring bud,
Actually, makes a sound so sweet?
Do you know that dripping springs,
Make a repetitive drummer's beat?

A humming bird bathing
And beating her wings,
Is actually a melody.
Nature abounds with these things!

Use your auditory imagination,
Conjuring up a symphony.
The music is all there just for you,
To put to your synchrony.

Our Love

To move is to speak,
To see is to hear,
To love is to learn
What the heart can bear;
Your heart, ours as one,
In the race towards where
The end will never come.

Our motion united,
Tells a thousand tales
Of warmth and riches,
Others can only dream about;
While we soar endlessly
In a clear blue sky,
And never have to wonder why.

To listen is to see
The wind in the evergreen tree,
That in its movement speaks
To you and to me;
And beckons us onward
To dreams not thought,
And melodies not taught.

Our time in space,
Ubiquitous by nature;
Our love, universal
As the universe itself,
Infinitely wrapping
Us in its complexity,
Nesting us in ubiety.

That place is here
Where we live,
See, move, love and hear
Our hearts murmuring,
Like a giddy brook,
As over the endless dreams,
It slowly, lovingly streams.

Unfinished

No other love hath I … ever,
Nor would it be within me to endeavor.
The heavens could not begin to conjure
Such a union … the Gods could not abjure."

Not 'Days of Wine and Roses'
Surely, I would want a beach,
 Gray skies, coolish wind, rolled up jeans,
Walking hand in hand, just being together.
Maybe not talking much,
Kissing slowly, bodies touching.

Afternoon mist arriving …
and then you are gone.
But the feeling of being with you
Has warmed my body.
It's there.

Just once more, together,
before we are not."

Musical Interlude

What joyous music
That reaches my ears.
Evoking sensations
Throughout the years..

The softness, the cadence,
The tone so true.
The soul receives
The senses from you.

The vocal movements,
The undulations.
The rhythmic swaying,
The orchestrations.

The tempo rises
To anticipated phrases,
Yet to be heard from;
Un-played places.

Adagio, allegro,
A symphony of sound.
Arias, sonatas,
Sensations abound.

Building, waning, waxing,
Intensity increases.
Crescendo crashing ...
Nothing ceases.

Rolling on and on and on,
Thunderous in your ears,
Yet, soft as eiderdown,
Hoping, the melody reappears.

And finally, the coda,
Once again!
A replayed melody,
Where and when?

Distant Love

As time slides by
And memories reminisce,
Warm thoughts linger
Amongst the autumn mists.

Thoughts like falling leaves,
Tumbling about in yester year,
Some vibrant, whose colors still exist,
Some as close as tomorrow, always to be near.

Unfulfilled wishes, consummated in time
By vicarious mental machinations.
Fleeting figments of the mind,
Achieved through sublimation.

Walks through life's vicissitudes,
A vacuum perceived or actual.
A dream of reality,
Ethereal, not factual.

Yet if stars cannot be touched,
Do they not exist?
Does the moon upon the waters,
Spawn temptations one can't resist?

Does distance lessen love,
Or are the bonds annealed?
Does insouciance prevail,
Or is the heart revealed?

Fate

A flooding deluge.
A river gone dry.
Man's emotions.
I wonder why?

Love, A Flower

For those apart,
A road of divergence.
Not unexpected,
Changing lives, emergence.

Beginning in propinquity
To an amorous attraction,
A crescendo evolving,
To an emotional exaction.

Once, two lives, hopelessly entwined
In impossible dreams.
Now contentment prevails
Through solo traveled seams.

Though paths crossed
Fleetingly, ore the years,
Profound feelings
Echo in my ears.

A humble gratitude
For a heart given,
From a soul soft and deep,
And an angel striven.

From an inner grace,
A song bird's voice,
A loving compassion,
A woman's choice.

Respect for exigencies;
Past cannot be present.
Sweet memories serene,
For images so pleasant.

Your life is yours
And mine is mine,
But better no doubt,
Than each other we did find.

A seed was sewn,
A blossom appeared.
A flower flourished,
The fragrance lasts for years!

Night

The dark slides in
As the light ebbs out.
Soon night critters
Will be all about.

Scratching, scurrying, wind on feathers.
Bright eyes reflecting the moon.
A hoot, a hiss, a growl, a howl,
Day-timers departing, not too soon.

A shadow darkens
Lunar light.
Opportunity knocks
For a nocturnal strike.

Some live, some won't, some eat, some don't,
A meal consumed, not in waste
As stealth is needed
For not a morsel to waste

A crunch, a thump
Why what was that?
Just a flying capture
By an omnivorous bat.

Night, a timorous time
And a balancing act
Between survivors
That have conjured a pact.

Rest ye though,
As the sun comes soon
And freedom's about.
All's at ease with nature's tune.

Sunrise

The golden eye of tomorrow,
racing through valleys,
over hilltops, through the trees,
driving out the dark;
Awakening every soul, saying,
"Wake up!" "Wake up!"
"I, the giver of energy, am here."

Shadows shrink in respectful play,
Some lingering, holding on
Before they will be whisked away,
To hide from day's passage.

Yawns and dawns,
Contagious, right to left, left to right.
Chromatic, purples, gold, yellows,
The spectrum of blended light.
From east to west,
God knows best
How to illuminate His land.

What mind could even try
To fathom the Majesty --
Veiled in clouded secrecy or
Beckoning us brilliantly:
"Follow Me!"

Unpredictability

I love your unpredictability,
Your spontaneity,
Your conviviality,
Your ability to love me so.

And let me tell you Dear,
There's one thing
That you make quite clear.
You're a delightful challenge to me.

Last Rose of Summer

I move now so very lightly to a soft fall breeze,
Watching my shadow on the wall.
Here with the sun – gone with the moon,
But a memory, lasts forever.

Petals burst with early Spring,
To be kissed by warmth and long hours,
To be nurtured as dreams,
To blossom with imaginative fantasies.

Blue skies, yellow petals, green stalks,
Or were they red with blushes of pink and white;
Perhaps a lavender juxtaposing to a Queen Mary,
Whose whiteness exemplifies purity?

Now the hues of a floral sunset,
Cast their waning moments
On those of like chromatic provenance,
Soon to slip to slumber.

My family is here in this garden of love,
Rainbow colors and fragrance of rapture.
We danced by day
And swooned by night.

Long melodies are seasonal.
Sleep is to rejuvenate.
Fear not, as cycles reappear;
We will return with unfolded glory.

Oceans of Emotions

Oh, my heart does sail with the waves,
Rolling in with such exuberance of emotion;
Ebbing, only to gather strength and rush on again,
Swelling, bursting, crashing with devotion.

How your voice lingers to urge me on;
How your presence surrounds me at every turning.
The softness of your wet caress
Leaves my body burning.

What magnificence is left as you wane away,
Your body undulating with a latent verve.
And with predictability your rejuvenated rise
To finalize your cycle on sculptured nerve.

Aegean Umbra Solis

The chiaroscuro of the Aegean afternoon light,
Drifting through slatted blinds on my heavenly wonder;
Transcending corporeal beauty
For the true love of soul.

The binding of two,
So meant for each other
That their spirits meld into one,
An amalgamation of union.

Music, wafting skyward,
Retsina, lingering in lip-embossed glasses.
Aegean blue – far below
You for me and I for you!

Autumnal Calling

The chill, whistling in from the north,
Remnants of nature's kaleidoscopic masterpieces,
Like birds fleeing south --
Finding their way for winter respite.

Mists still rising
As air and water equilibrate.
A veil to hide rough edges,
To wrap and soften the light.

A thin crust of resistant film
On standing still waters,
Slippery landing pads for migrating fowl --
All speak of dormancy.

But really?
I see a hare with tinges of white.
I see chickadees and meadow creatures,
And hear the crunch of big feet on brittle ground.

Why! It is just a changing of the guard,
A changing of ambiance,
A forthcoming whitewash,
To tidy things up a bit.

A phantasmagorical finish
To growth and expansion.
A well-earned rest,
To ponder perception.

Nap

The breeze stirs that rose,
On long stem dancing with the shadows.
The garden wall, so softly answers back,
While my loved one sleeps in sweet repose.

Her head tilted slightly,
A whisper of a smile across her lips.
What is she thinking,
As through her dreams she trips?

The music of memories past,
The sun, the stars, the moon?
Awaken she will,
Her reverie broken too soon.

Blue Moon

They asked me how I knew
Just when I knew I loved you.
To that I soon replied,

When her long legs I spied,
I therefore decried,
That she would soon be my bride.

Silence

"Silence is the ether of music."
Giscard d'Estaing: From a speech on silence, given at
The Ecole Normale de Musique in Paris

Silence sings a love song,
From Red Canyon to mountain wall.
From the scrub pine to the alpine,
Silence says it all.

Silence is caressing,
It soothes your mind.
Quietude for active thinking,
Someone special to find.

Silence can be everywhere,
It's for you to seek out.
It's the blessing of the countryside,
To find out what life's all about.

Silence is lost
In big city life.
Find out where it is,
To rid yourself of strife.

Silence is the serenity,
That clears the air.
Silence can be all about us,
Sometimes more than we can bear.

Silence is to live with.
Silence can make you strong.
Silence can be a panacea,
For all that seems to be wrong.

Silence, a beacon in the night,
It can follow you through the day.
Silence is absolutely necessary,
As it will light your way.

Prenuptial Doubts

Does a candle cast a shadow on the wall,
Does the flame leave an image at all?
Will love last with a tentative start,
A lasting imprint on a fragile heart?

Is a rose's red petal deliberately shed,
When fragrance is lost, no more to be said?
Is there a mind-of-a-kind to ultimately find
A guiding light to re-envision the blind?

Will the clouds drift away,
Or lingering, still make our day?
And will the sun still shine,
If our lives should intertwine?

Perturbations abound
Like echoes of sound,
Muddling, befuddling, cascading around;
Where's tranquility to keep feet on the ground?

Talk, converse, discuss and chat;
Senses won't cement just like that.
Similar foundations, a thread of commonality,
There has to be more to achieve rationality.

What bond then, what girder of strength
Will predispose our union to great length?
A cocoon is needed of warmth, love and security,
With impenetrable walls to guarantee purity.

Not much to ask you say?
Then make love go away.
Remove the senses from the mind.
Make life empty!

One More Time

I'd like the opportunity to take you to the top,
Let you down, oh so softly,
And then never, never stop.

To take you to lands where you have seldom been,
To sights, sounds and smells that only stimulate,
To vistas, valleys and mountains you've never seen.

Through a kaleidoscopic array of fantasies,
Those that leave indelible images
On your dreams to emote new choreographies.

Then on awakening, we plan again
To variants on themes just sung,
And as to how, where and when!

Súplica

If you can live with adulation
And not want the moon,
If you can endure admiration
And avoid a swoon.

If your life can be filled with affection
And you do nothing but want for more,
If you can turn into reality
The dreams that have gone before;

If you can live every day
As if there will be no tomorrow,
If you can push other's insults aside
And avoid the shadows of sorrow;

If you can subject yourself
To another one's love,
If you cannot lose sight of self
And accept guidance from above;

If you can look into my eyes
And see love as not seen before,
If you can understand
The depth of feeling and more;

If you can hold on
To the future at your fingertips,
If you can let me touch and touch again
The sweetness of your lips;

If you can envelope me
As I would you,
If our bodies can intertwine
And you realize my love is true;

If you can rise with me in crescendo
And live with me in passion,
If you can let angels touch your face
And sleep with me in satisfaction;

If all this seem foreign
Please don't let it be.
If you can somehow do these things,
Then the future is ours, for eternity.

No Limit

I'll love you till the world goes away.
My heart thrives on your heart's beat.
The earth rotates on our axis,
Branches sway to our dance,

Roses bloom, not per chance,
But because you are you;
And our romance.

And the Telephone Rings

And the telephone rings,
And the song bird sings,
And I dream all day
Of when that might happen.

Her voice to hear
Means she's somewhere near.
Her melody of life
Courses through my veins.

Her thoughtful sigh,
Her joyous cry
Of all that makes her happy,
And a tear of sensitivity.

What more than the sun to shine,
The moon beams so fine?
A whisper so tender,
A lullaby of sweetness.

A breeze through the pines,
Like poetic lines,
Define my life,
And my love for you.

Les Balons

Have you ever stopped to ponder
The ethereal way of the free balloon,
The effortless climb,
The unpredictable moves?

Not unlike love, hovering, moving,
Always dynamic,
Yet growing with familiarity
In what keeps it aloft.

A look, song, glance,
makes the heart soar,
New heights, greater vistas.
Can there be more?

Yes! As the horizon nears
With heights to be ascended,
Beauty seen and felt.
Raptures unending!

Fear

My ultimate fear that I live with every day
Is that in my worst nightmare you have gone away.
Where the confidence in love,
Shattered by history?

What to prevail to overshadow that harbinger,
A false credence that should not exist
Amongst daily proof of the antithesis.
Your love does in faith persist.

Morning Rise

Off to the lake they did flee
Cavorting about in nuptial glee.
To her fisherman's surprise,
T'was his love caught the morning rise.

With satisfaction imbued,
Somnolence ensued.
The moral of this *tail*,
You can fish without a pail.

So Simple

Mistletoe and snow,
Fall leaves all aglow.
I miss you so!

My Dream

I don't know where I will see you,
I'll see you in my dreams.
You've left my heart torn apart.
Now the end is near it seems.

Your touch a soft summer breeze,
Your kiss a sweet melody,
Your fragrance drapes over me;
Your voice, like a rhapsody.

You left me for whatever reason,
You left me with no Good Bye.
You left with no explanation,
You left me alone to die.

We were united as one,
We were so tied together.
We were solid, so it did seem,
We were soul mates forever.

And now it's over,
And what stays the same?
And what of us, my Dear?
And what if anything, remains?

I don't know where I will see you,
I'll see you in my dreams.
You've left my heart torn apart.
Now the end is near it seems.

Your window's closed to keep the bad air out.
Your door, tight shut, no opening there.
Your phone off the hook – just a busy signal.
Your mail unanswered, just not fair.

You took it all, your life and mine.
You went for a better dance.
You went to try to seek for more.
You never gave me a chance!

We could have made it.
We could have given it a try.
We never discussed it.
We never even asked why?

And is it all over now?
And the pieces, discarded dirt?
And the trail's end tomorrow!
And for no good reason, too much hurt.

I don't know where I will see you,
I'll see you in my dreams.
You've left my heart torn apart.
Now the end is near it seems.

Classy Girl

Got myself a woman.
She does not like to shop.
She ain't no shopping junkie,
No shopping till you drop.

The woman likes quality,
Special things for lots of money.
Please, no low-class items;
"Move that decimal over, honey."

A ride, she will decide
Would be better in a Ferrari.
A Ford will get you there, Baby,
But you'd always be sorry.

Trinkets are always appreciated
And flowers fade, my friend.
"You want time with me?
It's diamonds -- you must send."

Now flying is something special,
Comfort you can't barter.
She's always most relaxed
In her own private charter.

Fur coats, speed boats, castles with moats,
It's just a matter of taste,
Anyone can go for less.
Don't let better - go to waste!

Rembrandt, Renoir and Degas,
And she likes the performing arts.
A dullard she can't tolerate,
She needs a man with smarts.

Yes, the lady's unique.
A most beautiful girl.
She's one of a kind.
And she'll set your heart awhirl.

Behind every woman
There's going to be a tale
Some more interesting than others
Some'll make you pale.

Yeah! My woman's real classy
And that's OK with me
No need for someone else,
Don't want some new chassis.

A Spider's Web

A logical, methodical, expression
Of geometric, potential entanglement.
From its mystical, dew-shrouded morning-wonder,
To its purposeful sustenance management.

Each thread, a structural necessity,
Reparable with ease it would appear,
But timeliness is of the essence,
Les escapism, the creator might fear.

Such are the wonders of this world!
Embellishments for us to ponder;
While walking our tenuous threads,
As through life we wander

Snowy Fragrance

A snowy fragrance is ore the land
And all about us, clean.
Nature's housework is now done,
And all the land's serene.

The twigs and trunks are painted white,
The boughs bend low with cotton.
The earth, asleep under undulating folds,
Nothing has been forgotten.

As I look out upon this harmony,
I cannot help but ponder
What really wraps around us;
And in what direction will life wander.

Heaven is here -
But for us to ask.
The Lord has applied his art;
And in its beauty, we doth bask.

Beauty

Your beauty comes from all that surrounds us,
The earth, the sky, the sea.
And the absolute glory of it all
Is that your heart belongs to me !

Faith

He led me down His path.
Blindly, I followed along,
Attempting to do what was right,
Trying to be strong.

Faith, unmitigated as I went,
My love transcendent.
My life to finality,
Eternity, resplendent.

PaPa Joe's
A wonderful bar, up on stilts, Key Largo, FL

T'was down in the Keys, over on the West,
Fishin' with pros, you know, the best.
Surrounded by life, like in the Caribbean,
Characters, atmosphere, t'was a sight I was seein'.

Few boats below were tied up for the night,
The sun was setting. Oh! Such a sight.
Me and my wife, a woman to turn an eye,
Pulled out her chair, being a gentlemanly guy.

I strode up to the bar in that stilted shack,
Felt pretty damn good, just got back
From flats fishing, that's what I did;
All pumped up, this ole kid.

Kind a got sidewise, leaned on the rail,
Glanced down to spit, but there weren't no pail.
Looked at that Keep, right in the eye,
Held up three fingers, said "Believe I'll try" ….

In a gravelly voice, I proceeded to growl,
Pulled up macho from my inner bowel;
This had to be good, had only one shot.
Surrounded by locals, you know the lot.

Stranger there, they could tell,
Looking too good and a little too swell.
Well I took a deep breath and out it came,
A most God-awful moment … the sun was to blame.

"Tequila, Margaritaville and a good-looking' shill,
They'll get you every time.
Me, I like Ben Gay on the rocks …
With a whole lot a lime."

"Beg your pardon", the man did say,
Didn't quite hear you, **NO**! Don't go away".
I was exposed, it really was sad;
It was really awful, really that bad.

"Mount Gay, Sir", I meekly replied,
Wantin' to crawl back to my corner, wishin' I died;
"And please, a twist would be great."
Everybody heard, there was no escape.

Can You Handle That

Can you handle one that's never loved you more?
Someone that has never loved - that much before?
Are you ready for what tomorrow will bring,
A forever-life and an eternal spring?

Do you have any idea just what that means,
A love that is greater than all your dreams?
Can you handle that and never look back for more
On those that might have loved you before,

One that would put his life on the line
Just for you at any given time.
Your life is my life to have and to hold,
As no other love lives, till age grows beyond old.

Do you have any idea of just what you mean to me?
Are you blind to what others can plainly see?
Don't you realize what others lack?
Are you woman enough to handle that?

Little Woman

I know a little woman,
She ain't but five feet tall;
But when she snores in the bedroom,
The windows rattle in the hall.

Put her in the kitchen,
That's not her part ...
She can, if she wants,
Cook to break your heart.

She's bad,
She's mean,
She's a walkin', talkin'
Loving machine.

She's a horizontal lady,
That woman of mine.
Make a dead man groan,
And a grown man fine.

She knows how to get comfortable,
Just how to dress.
When I come home from work,
Better ... is far less.

You can't touch me,
When I'm by her side.
My feet don't hit the ground,
I got so much pride.

She's bad,
She's mean,
She's a walkin', talkin'
Lovin' machine.

She's a horizontal baby
That woman of mine.
Make a dead man groan
And a grown man fine.

If I were a snow flake

If I were a snow flake, I'd float near to you.
If I were a snow flake, I' be white against the blue.
There'd be no clouds up above
And I'd swirl around your love.

You cannot forsake
A snowflake like me,
Cause I am the finest one
You ever did see.

I'm part of your heart,
And part of your mind;
And never a finer snow flake, you'll find.

Others will melt and soon disappear,
But I'm indestructible,
And just get better
When you are near.

I think I will last forever you see,
Because you are my life;
And mean so much to me.

In Vain

Fragrance laden memories ....wafted
---sleepless moment.
So seductively subtle,
Imagination or supplication?

Dare to touch!
Alas!
Her mind elsewhere.

Celestially Speaking

Off all the heavenly bodies,
Why did my heart go out
To the furthest from earth's gravitational pull ?
Maybe because that's where the stars are brightest,
Beyond Orion, the Dippers and Taurus the Bull.

Brightest because they are unfettered
By pollutants thrown up by man.
Because they reflect the sun's true rays,
And not an abysmal lot of poppycock,
Or man's duplicitous ways.

Maybe its just because
That one wee star,
In all its splendor,
Lets me know who you are.

Just Italian

Three figs in the fountain,
Which one shall I eat?
Probably, none of them,
'Cause that's where they wash their feet.

Italy, the land that I love.
The wine they make with their feet.
They sing to you of amore,
And have way too much to eat.

To a beautiful young lady,
An Italian is the living end.
The rest of us are chopped liver.
We can't even pretend!

The Italian lovers,
Heroes sung of old.
Yet their population is shrinking,
And on their culture, we are sold?

They lie to you about their age.
With their mothers they are content to live.
"Itsa my villa, come over."
"The roof, it leaksa like a sieve."

They sing to you;
Arias and a sweet refrain.
Opera is in their blood,
The heroine, the villain, and "Oh the pain!"

Venice is sinking,
Pisa continues to lean.
Rome is in shambles;
And "Tourism" covers it with a sheen.

The Vatican is in disarray.
The Lire continues to buy less.
The Pope is next to God in demand,
But for a dollar, you can be blessed.

For many millennia,
They've managed to last.
They may exist in the present,
But they live in the past.

They thrive on lore,
It's with their hearts they live.
But they instill an inspiration,
And happiness they give.

Venture Out
Beautiful Amsterdam

The melodious rocking, creaking,
Rising from the canal below.
"Come roll in our craft as we ply
the waters in quest of life."

The aroma: baking, frying, roasting, grilling,
All stimulating gustatory delights.
Walk the edge, join the cacophony of awakening
To the dawn of evening being.

Linger not in your upstairs lair,
But come with me, now!
Time is fleeting, take my hand
As we explore mankind.

Autumnal Calling

The chill, whistling in from the north,
Remnants of nature's kaleidoscopic masterpieces,
Like birds fleeing south,
Finding their way for winter respite.

Mists still rising,
As air and water equilibrate.
A veil to hide rough edges,
To wrap and soften the light.

A thin crust of resistant film
On standing still waters,
Slippery landing pads for migrating fowl,
All speak of dormancy.

But really?
I see a hare with tinges of white.
I see chickadees and meadow creatures
And hear the crunch of big feet on brittle ground.

Why! It is just a changing of the guard,
A changing of ambiance,
A forthcoming whitewash,
To tidy things up a bit.

A phantasmagorical finish
To growth and expansion.
A well-earned rest
To ponder perception.

Supreme Power

Beauty starts with Nature,
And Nature never ends.
Man's nimiety, a dark cloud!
There will be no amends!

Arrogance unfettered!
Expiation, a vain attempt!
Creation of betterment?
Pathways to contempt!

A mere blip on horizons,
Insignificant, our lives.
Nature – the Supreme Power!
Time thrives!

Love: A Falling Star

Love can be like a falling star.
A wee bit of bright
In the middle of the night,
Intensifying explosively ...
And then out of sight....mmm!

Reasons

There's a blue moon shining ore my valley,
There'll be sunshine on me tomorrow.
Every day is a dream come true,
'Cause that's just the way it is,
When I'm with you.

There is a blossom on every hill,
And a song bird on every branch.
The mountain streams are running clear.
I feel your warmth when you're away,
And your love when you are near.

Your voice is like a serenade.
Your presence is my strength.
Your visage like everything beautiful,
Your tenderness a zephyr that caresses
....just a few reasons I love you so.

What Would I Do?

What would I do without my Dear, Dear Mary
To crawl up to me in the middle of the night,
To hold me tight, to deflate my anxieties,
To love me?

To feel my warmth and returned love,
To realize that she was safe.
Both to sleep again.

That words were capable of truly conveying,
A supplication unrealized.
Love, an impossibility without holism.

Our mutual entanglement
Of intertwining emotions.
A multiplicity of synaptic enhancements.

Sanibel Shells

The waves slip in and the waves slip out,
And in their passing, they leave no doubt
There will be one more pleasure,
And one more treasure.

A temptation to dart as it slides away,
Among its family in disarray.
It rolls, it turns and sheds its beauty.
Once so pure, it now completes its duty.

Reduced now to a grain, not so grand,
Yet dynamic still, as part of the sand.
And minerals left for others to use,
While we as humans must not abuse.

The story is there in every shell,
Look and listen to the story they tell.
As the waves slip in and the waves slip out,
The cycle of life it what's it's all about.

Under the Sun

In the shadow of the sun
Your love goes forth,
To caress those
That it touches.

Your eyes convey a
Warmth deep from within.
Your song, your voice, enchanted evening;
Time whiled, yet rushes by.

Too soon 'tis over,
Until next we meet.
Hold me again,
For our warm goodbye.

Importunity

What twist of fate!
A preemptive order ordained?
A Machiavellian duplicity,
An importune Diaspora to create ...

She went East, to the West went he.
He to shackling, ... to freedom she.
Her heart yearning; ... learning ...
That foolish chimera can
Only attempt to vicariously
Erase depth of distance, absence of touch;
Enable visual embrace, loved so much.

Laughter's sweet surround,
Tenderness prevailing,
Togetherness for the asking,

Compassion, availing.
A melody of chiaroscuro,
A canvas of harmony.

For love there's no definition
Without recognition
That divine cognition
Illuminates darkness!

Now, on hold,
Not to be bold.
Soon we grow old,
Tales to be told.
Time is fleeting!

Imagined exigencies
Maliciously designing,
Loathsome ...
"Cheval-de-frise!"

Erotica

Your sweet love flows ore my heart like honey!
The velvet of your touch burns into my soul.
Moon drops kiss the nape of your neck,
As you bend towards mine.

Your fragrance, a thousand flowers
Wafting on a summer zephyr.
Hushed tones, a mother to her young.
What enhancement could there be?
A comparison of none to thee!

Rekindle a Candle

You cannot rekindle a candle,
When the wick is not there.
You cannot pick a dream,
Right out of thin air.

A glass of wine is all but dead,
When there is no more nose.

And like a breeze that does not linger,
Out the window, love goes.

A few memories are all that is left.
High hopes dashed upon the shore.
What once was life itself ...
Alas, is no more.

Emotional Dynamism

Rivers of emotion,
Wide and deep.
A heart bursting with a longing
For a dream to keep.

Idleness spawns the ridiculous,
Truth and the obvious get twisted.
Reality fades,
In canyons misted.

Care and tenderness abound,
Eddying, back-flow, roiling, yet calm.
Joyous, bubbling, pervasive music,
Captivating ... right in your palm.

Look far as the river tumbles,
Gathering strength through the sands.
Ask not, but trust
In gathered vigor through the lands.

She's strong, vibrant,
A mind of her own to keep.
No control
It's her way to seek.

Emotions must move,
Stagnancy means rot.
Energies move on,
Channeled, better than not.

Directed to common cause,
One can only pray.
Vitality lies in love's volume,
Singularly directed at the end of the day.

Absence

To miss one's true love,
Is not to sleep;
But to ache
And perhaps to weep.

To see the day break,
Yet 'tis dark, life without, droll;
And the moon, though full,
Shows only a glimmer on the soul.

The melodious of tunes
Well the eyes with tears.
You possess yourself with work,
To escape loneliness and fears.

When comest thou
Back to my arms,
Most lovely of all roses,
To release both from harm?

My heart will beat again
To your pulse of love,
Always to recognize,
A gift from above.

A Wave

Love comes gently,
Swelling to the heart's beat,
Like a wave rising to its feet.
Momentum grows, crescendo builds.
The shore looms - combers roil.
Emotional exhilaration!
Physical exultation!
Slowly evanescing -
The ebb is near,
Waning - inevitable return.
Each a little different.
An effervescent love –
Always there.

Contemplation

September of 1997 while walking on Dell Mar beach.
(Four Parts) "Pre-marital Questions"

Thought One:

Could you love a man
Just because he's faithful, true and trustworthy,
And poured your love back to you ten-fold,
And not have love predominantly based on sex?

Could you love a man
Who respected you, honored you,
And wanted to do things with you,
The whole day through;

And let yourself be loved
As no man has ever loved you before,
Without putting the physical as the highest priority,
And yet letting the cards fall where they do?

Could you allow the rest of your life to be so secure
That you knew exactly where love was coming from,
And feel totally at ease,
While you're apart?

To accept that man
And not be selfish about his love for his family,
As long as you knew
You were the highest priority.

Could you be by his side
And not covet those younger?
Could you accept what he provided
And not want for more, if plentiful?

That's a tall order when all around you
Others are trying to lead you astray.
Can you recognize that you'll have, they have not
Except for a fortunate few.

If you can,
My Dear Mary,
Then that's why I can -
Love you.

You are right for me,
Dear Love,
In so many ways
But, am I right for you?

Thought Two

I want to spoil you.
I want to give you
What you haven't had.

Not material riches,
But you being able to be totally dependent
And yet maintain your independence,
Being "Mary" and true to yourself and your goals.

I can be a one-woman man,
Can you be a one-man woman?
Or are your needs
More than I can provide

Thought Three:

What creature I, could possibly aspire,
To set a goal so high,
That in all probability it's unattainable;
But yet, I have to try.

And who might I be,
To glory in thee?
Ah! What utter presumption,
And for the world to see.

Am I really the man,
With the proper élan,
To pull this off?
I think I can!

All it takes is verve,
And a degree of nerve,
And a lot of lady luck,
To let me to win this serve.

But try I must,
Lest this encounter be a bust;
And the shocking truth
Leaves me totally in disgust.

<u>Thought Four:</u>

What a lovely angel
Has come into my life
To remove the stress, turmoil and strife.
A loving hand, a soft touch,
It is more that I could want by Oh, so much!

One-Under
Dr. Roger Broderson and a golf course at White Bear Lake, MN.

Roger tried
And Roger damn near died.
White Bear "Fifteen"
Was everyone's nemesis.
Par it and the "Club" will think you lied.

A hogback going in.
Pitches to the left,
Also to the right.
Miss and you double digit.
"Hit it straight, you mental midget"

I'm sure there's more,
A special hole here and there.
Any money on them,
And they'd give you quite a scare;
But that makes this diabolical game ... really quite fair.

For you see,
It ain't just you and me,
There's a whole slew of players who try
And most of them just give up and die.
It's only those with the right stuff,
Who can pound out of the really tough rough.

So just keep on swinging,
Never stop singing.
Hammer at that game you love,
And you're likely to finish your day
"One under" ... on the man above.

Diminishing Return

A glimpse at the future,
Reflections on the past.
Is it possible for one to succeed
While the latter did not last?

Will the future remain secure,
Will clouds fade away?
Will the vision that we have together ... stay?

Will the moments of anticipated delight,
Awaken with the dawn?
Or become obscure,
In the night?

Will our rain drops be always pure?
Will our mountains be soft and mellow?
Will the sunshine be warm and soothing?
Will we each retain our allure?

The cost of finding out is time.
Which truly has to be spent.
To make sure our quest is each other,
The attraction, heaven sent.

I Miss You

How I miss you,
How I wish I were there,
The feel of your fingers,
Running through my hair.

Your style,
Your grace.
Your presence
In every place.

You are me,
I am you.
Without, I am nothing.
Together --- cemented as two.

The Question

Are you two ready for the kind of love
That does not warm with the morning sun,
Because it transcends solar energy,
To give you love's deep warmth ...
The whole day through?

Are you ready for the ubiquity
Of love's envelope,
So that you feel its strength
and gentle guidance ...
The whole day through?

Are you ready for the feelings
That unite all the myriad facets of love,
And yet manifest the wisdom,
And maturity of experience...
The whole day through?

Are you prepared to love in return,
Someone who gives their life to you,
Unequivocally and forever,
And never look back ...
The whole day through?

Are you prepared to live
In a cocoon of security,
Knowing that your emotional
And physical needs will be met ...
The whole day through?

Are you prepared to accept
What is being given to you,
And not squander your thoughts on frivolity,
Yet languish in its luxury ...
The whole day through?

If you truly are,
Then move
To the horizons of tomorrow,
Where the yesterdays dwindle
As a fading glimmer of memories.

If you truly are,
Then let the sunset of today
Be the sunrise to eternity,
And let your love be perpetuated
By all that is beautiful and true.

And say to each other –
Come! Rise with me in crescendo,
Love me with passion.
And may a thousand angels caress your face
While you sleep with me in satisfaction.

Gray Titans

Ethereal rays to placate gray titans!
Heaven's attempt on restoration,
An eonic endeavor,
For earth's perturbations

Away

There's a purple haze in the canyons,
As the day draws to a close.
The roses' heads are all nodding,
As they head towards sweet repose.

But even though there is beauty,
There is something very amiss.
My dear love is not with me,
And it is emptiness that I must kiss.

There's a palpable absence,
A soundless roar.
My life is agitated,
With loneliness, I abhor.

But the saving grace is time
As I know she shall return.

My Love

My independence is waning,
You have become so much a part of me
Through these years.
Can you not see?

These tiring last years
Have affected me so.
How I love you,
Do you not know?

Everything I try to do,
To show you how much I care,
Every moment of my life.
Are you not aware?

I cannot describe
What you mean to me.
A loving guiding light,
An angel for eternity.

A breath of fresh air each morning,
A day fulfilled each night.
The little sounds you make,
In hilarity or fright.

Oh Lord, my Dearest One,
Please let me not fail
To show love at all times,
As to our horizons we sail.

Soft as Velvet
A long-lost love

You say the right things,
But you don't mean what you say.
Your words are as soft as velvet,
But they'll soon go away.

You say that you love me,
But that's not true.
That we'll spend our time together,
Until our lives are through.

Your words are as soft as velvet
But they don't mean what they say.

I Guess, Kinda, Maybe

I guess, kinda, maybe,
I looked into her eyes.
"The two of us could be we",
I said much to her surprise.

Thus, our lives began.
She had a love for all,
More than I could understand,
All creatures, great and small.

And to our lives there crept
Small young ones wee;
Such joy, we often wept,
A glorious sight to see.

And then those little ones,
To grownups they grew,
And had daughters and sons;
And like chaff before the wind, they blew.

And now we sit and dream awhile,
And watch the days slip by.
We lived and loved in style,
And now listen to the evening breezes sigh.

They tell a sweet tale
Of two souls grown to one,
Of two lives, a union, n'ere to fail,
Of wild flowers beneath the sun.

Lives, like flowers,
May blossom and flourish;
Yet they too must fade 'round the bowers,
Memorable fragrances, for others to nourish.

"Well, I guess, kinda, maybe,"
I looked into her eyes;
"The night is near, you can see,
To bed! – for tomorrow we must rise."

Les Montagnes

Mountains, who is not to say that that they are not my nirvana?
A geomorphological manifestation on this orb where we exist,
Where you look forward to hearing your heart pound,
And the ensuing reverberations within your mind.

What greater grandeur could there possibly be,
Lofting your spirits to the heights of reality.
Piercing the skies with dark, white, gray, green, and blue.
They allow you to soar with the eagles, to be free in body and spirit.

Their accoutrements, soft as newborn moss, fierce as diamonds,
Whet your mind like nothing else could ever endeavor.

A reincarnation of a stagnant soul,
Mental and physical rejuvenation.
All you could dream for!

Thoughts

The fragrance of wet sage wafting over the hills,
The cockerel's call in the distance, heralding morning,
The coyotes mournful wail, leaving the night before,
Just a bare few of my truly coveted feelings,
That make all of nature, the supreme power.

The impossibility of accurately defining that magnificence,
The absurdity of absenting one's self from all that surrounds them,
The arrogance of stating they know nature,
The hubris in the assumption that they can somehow rise above her,
Result in the making more minuscule, mankind's intelligence.

Why then do we try to exercise our in ingrained egocentricities?
Why do we do our utmost to destroy what is naturally given to us?
Why then do we disguise this reprehensible effort
Underneath platitudes and meaningless, weak, efforts?
Is it to assuage the reality of our true inferiority?

Eonic history to those that follow, should there be any,
Will show their predecessors were contemptuous of Nature's ways,
That their rapacious efforts resulted in the nudation
Of what once was a newly bountiful planet;
Destroyed Earth's preeminence in our known universe.

Being a Zephyr

What freedom a zephyr!
A wiggle, a jiggle,
A perch upon a branch.
Gently rippling a pond
Making a rose swoon
Tickling a dandelion,
Watching the seeds drift.

Changing a butterfly's direction
Nudging a maiden's tresses
Supporting a hummingbird's wing
Caressing a bee's knees
Helping a Mayfly aloft
Carrying melodious notes
Wafting a delicious fragrance
Hiding in a shadow
Kissing the cheek of a loved one
Being ornery with carefully placed feathers
Dancing with softly falling rain droplets,
Melding with others to slowly grow,
Morphing out of your mukti,
A gentle bye-bye until next time.
What joy!
Just think how much fun
You might have
being a breath of a zephyr.

Part 2 … Family Endearments

Genealogically Speaking
Written for Carol Wood and Charles Duell's rehearsal dinner, 9/1963

If you should drop the titles
Such as in-laws, steps and halves,
You'd find a funny family
And one that's full of laughs.

I've got cousins by the dozens
And brothers four or more;
Sisters two or three
No more! Please, I implore..

My cousin says he'll soon be my brother
And my sister will soon disappear.
She says that she's soon my cousin
And of that she'll have no fear.

Now according to geometry,
She will be my little brother,
'Cause things equal to the same thing
Are equal to each other.

Now my cousin's future wife's oldest brother
Has my youngest brother's oldest niece with him.
A fact that she's not present now,
Certainly, is a sin.

Madam's youngest's oldest's sister,
Is just half our reason here.
If it weren't for Reverend's oldest brother's son,
This whole thing would be sort of queer.

Mother's sister's oldest brother
Is my sister's future husband's dad
And he's just part behind this party,
For which we are so glad.

Now Grandma's eleventh great-grandchild's aunt
Was just that sort of girl,
To attack her eldest brother's younger cousin
And set his heart a whirl.

But he responded in double-quick time;
And the way the jet age is,
Between France, U.S., Spain and others,
He is soon to make her his.

Now to write one's family tree
Takes a great amount of push,
But not even the best of us
Could paint this bramble bush.

To go on and on this way
Would just confuse you more.
Tune in tomorrow
And you're bound to know the score.

So stand up now
And let's say with sincerity,
God bless them both ...
May they have peace, happiness and prosperity.

Sister Dear
On organizing a family reunion

You're a sister, daughter, cousin, mother.
Can't have everything your way,
You're not my brother.

But what you are, Dear Sister,
Is a whirling dervish.
Try to call you, "Darn, I missed her."

To your mother, you're a darling daughter.
From time to time she wishes,
You should do as you aughter.

To your own, you are a mother.
Your wish is their command
And not something other.

And to your mother's son, your brother
He's very happy that you shouldered a load
Under which, he' probably smother.

To a number here, you are a cousin,
Who are glad that there is one of you,
And not a dozen.

But what all of us really want to say
Is thank God,
This reunion went your way.
You're a planner, impresario and statistician,
An instigator, agent and part magician.
A traveler, companion and part-time vet.
In your ways, you've had to be set.

You're an improviser, organizer, strategizer and cajoler
Immovable like a molar.
You're an enigma not an anathema.
You have charisma, but no plasma.
You're a calculator, masticator, eructator, flatulator,
Perpetrator director and actor.
Administrator, recreator, promulgator and prestidigitator,
Manipulator, cogitator and placator and character.

Is there no end to this logorrhea?
Not really, its just oral diarrhea.

Sis and we hope that this endeavor is giving you as much
pleasure as it is giving all of us.
We Love you !!!

The Man from Wyoming
To brother Willis on his 60th

Back in forty-four,
At the end of the war,
Something happened way out in the West.
His mother wasn't quite sure
And his father became insecure,
As to just what would be this boy's quest.

When young, he had friends galore,
But he seemed to long for more,
And turned his eyes to sheep.
That was his cerebral undoing,
His activity ungluing,
And caused the rest of the flock to weep.

When graduating Fountain Valley,
He was urged not to dally,
So, with a girl, started a conversation.
He immediately became affected,
But the girl got dejected
Cause oration exceeded duration.

At University he succeeded
In acquiring only what he needed,
A diploma without Cum Laude.
But he graded the maids,
As he made his grades,
And all without becoming too rowdy.

"I'll try pictures instead
Of women lying in bed",
His musings caused him to think.
And develop them he did,
But those photos he hid,
As in reflection, they caused him to drink.

Then, with barely a glance,
There were ranches by chance,
And all the ensuing glory.
But that got stale
On the hot dusty trail,
Out in ole Dayton and Story.

But he tried as he might,
And he finally got things right;
Moral pluralism was over.
With children two …
As far as he knew,
There was no longer a need to be a rover.

He used to walk tall,
Or sometimes to crawl,
When navigation proved incomplete.
And with a mind not too refining,
And not set on defining,
There's no telling with whom he would meet.

Now he reflects, as do others,
All fathers and mothers,
Just what parenting does entail.
There's ups and downs
And rounds and rounds,
But the love will always prevail.

So, the years go by
In the twinkle of an eye,
And you do just what you must do.
You work and you frolic,
And come down with colic,
And bemoan those lost, that you knew.

Now he sits tall in the saddle,
'Cause that's all he can straddle;
His arthritic knees can't bend.
His back is lordotic,
And his neck is kyphotic,
But he'll die trying … right up to the end.

He's a sexygenarian
And a complete contrarian,
And his hair is damn near gone.
But give him time,
Lest he feel too sublime,
With his undying love for Dawn.

So that's the story of t he man from Wyoming,
Who had his heart set his heart on roaming;
He's now considerably older.
You used to hear him complain,
Now you just hear him strain;
All he wants now … is just to hold her.

But I got to say before I am through,
That younger brother, I look up to you;
And I know we're not of the same mother.
But we got the blood of our father
And it doesn't take much bother,
That for a brother, I wouldn't take
Any other!

Ah, The Memories!
To my dear cousin Jeanie, who introduced me to Paris

The first time I saw Paris, I was there with you
Your concierge "Ne quite pas", just wouldn't do.
I'd hang up and wait for later and hope that you'd be in.
Your patience and teaching helped me make it through.

When I think of France, I think of you
Raising just a few eyebrows amongst those we knew
For the things we did together,
But conscience was clear, though thoughts were far from few.

When I think of Switzerland, I think of you.
The gendarme stopped us and "Ne parle pas Francais"
was all I knew,
And left it all up to my linguistic travel-mate
To sort and fix things as she knew so aptly how to do.

When I dwell on the finest cuisine ever experienced,
My first squab in a café overlooking Lake Lucern,
(Maybe it was "Geneva – doesn't rhyme) It was all exquisite.
The bill was my main concern.

And then the crossing of the border –
An outhouse of an inspection point,
The agent madly waving -
My non-stop at that inconspicuous joint.

Memories are all we have,
But ain't they great!
Let the lesser ones – the negatives,
Fall through the grate.

And so Dear Jeanie,
Life consumes us in most delightful ways.
Time passes too quickly.
Enjoy your days!

"Vive dum vivos!"
Live while alive!
"Vis Vie"
Live life

On Occasion
Thank you!

The pine needles are resting easy,
The dust has settled down.
Eaton's has returned to normal,
The clan is not around.

The raucous cacophony
of the ubiquitous children
is open to conjecture,
whether from He, She, of Them.

The leaves start to fall,
Twisted, warped, seemingly in shock.
Is it attributable to the tribe,
Or the seasonal clock?

What was it that happened?
Was it something malicious?
Or was it simply the actions
of those capricious?

I would venture
In complete sobriety
to most emphatically state,
There was no impropriety.

Then what was,
was what?
There were impressions that will linger
and thoughts not abrupt.

There were the revelations
That the world for real
Was not made of chaos,
But did allow man to feel.

There were fleeting moments
On the mountain top or on the green
Where our hearts were not truly ours,
But unstoppable, like the riffles on the stream.

With a tenuous, precarious hold on reality
Waiting to sway,
To be moved to greater dreams,
or eddy around in mock play.

And this inner realignment,
As it were,
Gave us a chance to think
And to defer.

The monumental weights
Peculiar to each one,
But when compared to those of others,
Seemed like hardly none.

The confrontations with dejection,
The bottomless pit of abject depression,
Priorities, practicalities, principles or prudence
All a matter of question.

But not one without solution,
Not without persistence;
All made entirely possible
By a Super Power existence

And what a more perfect place,
Amid the grandeur of Wyoming solitudes,
To contemplate and reflect
On nature's vicissitudes.

Or to linger a moment
At spectrum's opposite end
And remove yourself from a preconceived plateau,
The inalienable right you were willing to defend.

And realize that perhaps a lower self-perception
Is one you should seek,
And consort if you will
With the humble and the meek.

There were the nostalgic memories
Of time gone by
That elicited wistful glances
And a heartfelt sigh.

However, with a new day
And a brighter sun
Our thoughts went forward
To work not yet begun.

But one Glory of man
Is that he is blessed with the wisdom to think back
When haunted by seemingly unsurmountable problems,
Can stop, ponder, reflect and retrack.

To those moments
in the summer of Seventy-three
And to the two that made it happen;
Mind-straightening, emotion-smoothing serenity.

The logistics, the planning and diplomacy,
Exasperations, expenditures and preparedness,
By two who epitomize
Unselfishness,

There is a beautiful way to do things
And a wonderful way to go,
And a magnificent place to do it in,
And a lasting indebtedness to those you know.

A place out beyond ...
Up over, ... or back there.
It's a memory we will cherish
And be thankful in our prayer.

Our gratitude is deep
For activities extracurricular
And our love is sincere
For one in particular.

JCB On Ninetieth

We know Aunt June as:
An inner soul that warms
to embrace all that she touches.
One who has an outward presence
that belies the physical turmoil beneath.

As unassuming as the blossom
that opens its petals each day
to the life of the sun.

As unselfish as the rose
that gives all to the passer-by,
yet folds at the end of its day,
only to rise anew and keep on giving.

What allegiance does this mortal have
with the Omniscient?
He who hath put earth,
sky and heaven together.
To have, we must but ask.
Perhaps it is as a child of God,
in whose loving grace, she doth bask.

Part 3 … Emotions to Mother
Mother's birthday and her final demise.

Mother at 90, April 7, 2000

The English tongue is a rich one!
Create any tapestries under the sun,
Chase squirrels or just go nuts.
Get lost at little cost
And obfuscate with ands ifs or buts.

But if you stop to ponder
What's way out yonder,
In this land of endless semantics;
You can understand what makes this land,
And why it's great for romantics.

We need a way
To describe the lay,
Of the people we love the most.
Whether mother, brother, sister or other,
Or perhaps even our host.

So, listen if you will,
And try and keep still,
As I attempt a limited description.
An ovation, laudation, miniscule summation,
And hopefully accurate depiction.

Mother she is, and always will be.
That is obvious as anyone can see,
And her many attributes are evident.
If politics were just,
She'd be our next president.

One-word signs would appear all over,
Xanadu to Timbuktu to Kathmandu, Calcutta,
The Horn and back to Dover;
The truth would prevail!
Affirmations undeniable,
Verities, ...   against which no one could rail.

Enough introduction,
Which is devoid of corruption;
This deity we must describe,
Devine and sublime,
And not susceptible to bribe.

A lady, not shady,
A dancer, a prancer,
A sailor, prevailer and tailor.
A controller, paroller, cajoler,
Resolute like a molar.

A leader, a feeder, never a pleader,
A healer, an appealer, and dealer,
A believer, retriever and super achiever.
Statuesque, picturesque, even arabesque.
Reliable, one whose muliebrity is undeniable.

A planner, impresario and statistician,
An instigator, agent and part magician,
A traveler, companion and mate,
With a curiosity impossible to sate.
A talker, a walker, never a bawker.

A tryer, a flyer, a plyer, not a crier,
An improviser, organizer, strategizer,
Adjudicator, perpetrator, director and actor,
Administrator, recreator, promulgator, prestidigitator,
Cogitator, placator and character.

Lest you think I'm delirious,
I'll now get serious
And really tell it like it is.
As a nonagenarian and all of the above,
Mother, you're so easy to love.

Happy Birthday!

Dissynchrony
Gangrenous pathology – etiology, poor circulation

Have you ever stopped to think what effort it took
To disguise that look
About just exactly what you saw?
Or for that matter,
When among you friends you gather,
Indulge in idle chatter about how you felt about it all?

That your pain
Is only dulled by the shock upon your brain.
That you have to feel, hear, and see this every day,
That no matter what people think,
No matter what you drink,
The vision is there to stay.

> *Oh, this martini is delightful"*
> *Now let me tell you something frightful.*
> *My Mother's foot is rotting away.*
> *"Try one of these morsels,*
> *The taste of Blackened Red Fish,*
> *Or these little burned sausages here, a tasty dish.*

Quite right, color of gangrene you might say.

> *Yes, it started with her toes,*
> *Exact idiopathy, nobody knows,*
> *The doctors call it peripheral vascular disease.*
> *Here comes Eleanor Mead*
> *She'll talk your head off, take heed.*
> *We'll regale her with some pathology*
> *And disrupt her ease.*

And so you blather and no one begins to understand
What this all entails,
And how your emotions you must command.

STOP! And think for a moment or more.
Where would your emotions be?
Are you really so insensitive you cannot see?
Is it fear of reality that makes you ignore?

Who is that woman lying there
With her leg protruding in the air?
Doctors and nurses gather near;
They studiously examine the rotting tissue
And proclaim, expecting no issue,
We must amputate, will it be here or there.

That decaying, ulcerating, odorous foot you see,
At the moment does not belong to you or me.
It's remote, disjointed pathology that belongs to another.
But look again,
My educated friend,
For that pained and loving creature there,
Could be your mother.

She's mine!
And now I have to try and find
That inner strength
To make her feel she is not alone;
When, inevitably, she's to lose that bone.
To make her feel loved at any length.

What I am saying, don't misconstrue,
I must do what I must do.
I join the ranks of the others,
Who, as they gain maturity,
Are given some surety
That they will aid the passing of their mothers.

It's a heavy honor that we must accept,
Hoping that we can be reasonably adept
In understanding their physical and psychic pain.

It's with patience that we must let them travel,
Their mental ramblings to unravel;
Though dubious, in strength, I guess we gain.

Her horizons creep inexorably and painfully near.
Her past races to the present, poignantly clear.
Her memories descend on her with increasing rapidity,
Trying for one last time to relive life vicariously,
And walk that fine line
Between here and there ... precariously.
Remember the pleasant, live with laughter, avoid acerbity.

And then her purposeful decline hits the stumbling block.
She is belted with something
That should not precede the clock.
What equanimity she might have had,
Is now taxed beyond all boundaries of propriety,
And imbues her fading mind with anxiety.
And instead of dwelling about the good,
She gets to dwell on the bad.

Such perfection, her life;
Nary aberrant periods of strife.
Blessings, all so gracious.
Events, predictably synchronous.
Circumstances, propitious.
Nothing unusually audacious.

I'm sure she asks herself if this is a normal life's end ...

> *What grievance did I perhaps not amend?*
> *What did I do in yester year*
> *To bring about this fear that trembles my mind?*
> *I want to leave all that behind.*
> *Give me peace with death being near.*

Like the tide, ebbing and returning, my resolve
To face the decisions that must evolve.
Where's the fortitude that was such a part of me?
My humor wanes,
My energy drains.
Such ignominy!

If there is mercy, my heart
Which had such a strong start
Would cease at night.
No pain,
No strain.
Eternal light.

And so you think, *There but for the grace of God go I.*
You are right. You could be, what meets the eye.
It is your mother's plight and there will be no forum!
You go forth and attempt to nullify your sensitivity.
You try to categorize emotions with objectivity,
So that you may cope with a modicum of decorum.

While Waiting (2-05-03)
Patiently in hospital - thoughts

How could anyone as protected as she
Hope to envision and see
The worlds of others,
Sisters and brothers
And the likes of you and me.

***

We had a lunch date, but, Alas!
She had a heart attack and almost passed.
But she stabilized and then,
Started all over again.

*** (Perhaps Mother's thoughts ...)

This time? Next?
Leaves me perplexed.
This waiting game,
Each time the same.

Fear and then red lights.
In the day or in the night.
And then stabilize.
The meaning – must rationalize.

Oh, be still my heart
Until death do us part.
How should I grieve
About how I should leave?

Your way is not mine,
But I accept it as such.
Be gentle, be kind,
Caress softly my mind.

Hay, you at arm's length.
Do you really have the strength
To be by the side
Of someone who died,
When that someone is your mother?

Where were you
When the fingernails went blue?
Or the Chain-Stokes breathing
Sent your heart seething,
Because there was nothing you could do.

It's a test under fire,
When there is no one to hire
To bolster your reserve,
And give you enough nerve
To see you through the emotional quagmire.

***

And so I leave her with everything unsaid,
Lying there in that hospital bed.
Not entirely procrastination,
Nor reticent articulation.
It's just that in her era, less said the better.
Not appropriate, the tongue to unfetter.
And so "I love you" is not declared.

The mind is not prepared
For abnormal social priorities,
To which are attached anxieties.

> *The doctors were amazed,*
> *As into my eyes they gazed.*
> *Too many V-tach's, to my son they said,*
> *As they scrutinized instruments they read.*
>
> *My inner self said, "To hell with them,*
> *I'll recover once again.*
> *Amount of time I have is my prerogative.*
> *Not their timing, interrogative"*
>
> *My heart belongs to me.*
> *It is not for them to see.*
> *It's my decision, not theirs,*
> *As to when I climb the stairs.*

I may not have control of the wheel,
But I'll be damned if I'll let them steal
My right to live or die,
Recover, or even try.

I am the captain of my fate,
The master of my soul.
What is to be
Is up to me.

***

Hey you out there,
What's that sound?
All you heirs,
Gather around.

She is gone
And maybe there'll be
Something for you,
Something for me.

Well don't be too greedy.
You are not really needy.
And I'll dispense,
When it makes sense.

She made her wishes known
Long before she came to my home.
Her will may give you pause.
Her desires were for a cause.

***

From the hospital I shall go,
These portals no more to know.
She passed the test,
Knowing now, she's at rest.

***Yonder beacon beckons,
Without which I cannot reckon
Which road I should take,
Lest I make a big mistake.
It makes little difference now
So take either for heaven's sake.

Like the Phoenix she has arisen
From incarceration and prison.
She goes with pride,
Having never broken stride.
She stood by the main mast,
Not the mizzen.

She leaves in her wake
Her own personal rake,
And tales of enjoying her life.
She's paid for the tune
And has danced 'neath the moon.
And strove to be a good wife.

This lady of lore
Has sailed from shore to shore,
And nary a port did she miss.
If it was under the sun,
Then it was meant for fun.
Her way, she did insist.

So, we must say good-bye,
And never ask why
She did things the way she did.
A lady of surprises,
She saw few demises,
And did just what her will did bid.

Until Death Do Us Part

The telescoping of reality,
The immediacy of mortality;
A blessed somber event.
Your feelings unknown to the extent
Of just how far they can be stretched,
Beyond the bounds of normality.

Dichotomy and ambivalence,
Yet making perfect sense.
Relief and grief,
For a life not brief.
Questions and answers,
To be pondered in your mind.

Time will ameliorate most
By the ultimate Host.
She must fly!
But still, "If only I had..." and "Why?"
She let go, we must now;
And move on as would be her wish.

A Lady's Grace

Too soon the cloak of finality,
Too swift the angel's wing.
Our hearts, mere moments in reality,
Heralding the gates of heaven to bring
Our souls upward and outward,
Our memories for bells to ring.

But for providence we join with those
Whose lives less fortunate carry that fate.
Masters of life while given,
Striven to balance and equate
Beatitudes so cherished by others,
And themselves recognized too late.

Part 4 … To have and to hold
Remembrances … thirty-five-year marriage … drunk driver victim

Just for You

Glowing ember with warmth, just out of sight,
Waiting the soft zephyr to make it alight.
Cradled by memories of yester year,
Yet feeling presence, oh so near.
It smolders on in perpetuity,
Always a yield from a love annuity.

Its destiny to remain a beacon in the night,
To enfold with sensitivity all that was right.
It glows with a tenderness, caressing years gone by,
And is energized by never asking why.
The ember of love persists through time,
An enveloping dream of hearts entwined.

I Remember

I remember the moonlight
On rippled waters far below.
I remember the sounds of memories,
Of long, long ago.
I remember a special place
Where we were one,
Face to face,
One soul, one kiss for a life time,
Of remembered bliss .

I remember voices,
That to us were unique,
But in actuality, of love they did speak.
Of a love transcending anything we knew.
Only in retrospect, can we barely
Surmise what in reality it did mean.
Two souls wedded in harmony,
That only Gods dare speak of,
For mortals can only dream,
Of such a union here on earth.

Or were we here, did we feel,
Touch, caress, smell each other's fragrance of love?
Was it real or only imagined?
Full meaning then,
May escape us now,
But metamorphosed over time
Brings smiles to our brow.
As life may be better somehow,
Dreaming the dreams of young lovers,
And knowing that it was real.

Real enough to warm our hearts,
and yearn for more,
Knowing that what will evolve,
Will be better, deeper, more fulfilling,
Than those wondrous moments passed.
Face to face then,
Now soul to soul.
Our lives as one
To become parts molded into a whole.

Back Then

It was a rainy week in December,
Or maybe September,
... I don't really remember when.
We walked and talked and laughed a lot ... back then.

Sodden and damp we settled in by the fire,
Steam rose from the dogs' furry coats.
The hot toddy was soothing,
... as the flames crept higher.

I reminisce as if you were here,
... because I guess you are.
At least in my mind;
... It all seems so clear.

Why did you have to leave,
... it just isn't fair?
I live and dream our memories,
... and in between I still grieve.

I Used To Sing

I used to sing,
Now I sigh.
I used to dance,
Now I cry

She left me one Spring
Without a chance to say goodbye.
No last kiss ... her heart just stopped.
Resuscitate ... they could only try.

Head lights blinding.
"They're in our lane."
Nothing to remember, only the pain,
Then the realization ... and more pain.

Crashing windows! People all around!
I held her mangled beautiful hand;
The hand I fell in love with forty years before;
The last image of her, the hand,
with the wedding band.
Life in vain ... and more pain.

She'll never leave me for I can't let her go.
Sounds of a door shutting, a moment to share,
The subtlest feeling ...
And she is always there.

Her life spent loving!
Death without dignity!
Talents wasted for what cause?
A mere blip in time,
But affecting so many.

There Was A Time

There was a time when first I cast eyes on you,
That I knew we'd be inseparable,
That I knew we'd be for each other,
As the moon and stars are to the night.

That was a time when my heart burst forth,
My every moment, a moment of your life.
Your touch, your voice, your every move,
Devoured insatiably, to be filed in my memory.

There was a time when we woke up together,
To treat each day as a new beginning.
There was a time that the rising sun was ours alone,
Lighting our day, showing our way, our hearts intertwining.

There was a time when each second, of every day and year
Was the connection holding us together,
To love each other as if there were no tomorrow;
To travel through life, so much joy, little pain and sorrow.

There was a time when life could be no better,
When life was the air that we breathed;
When life was all that surrounded us,
When life was made of love.

So bonding, so secure that nothing could invade our realm.
Our perfect world, the envy for all to see,
Except for my blindness, the fact it could all end so quickly;
In a heartbeat of fate, that could take you from me.

Oh, for that time like it was in the beginning,
When two hearts were welded together,
When life's pathways were lined with flowers,
When hurdles were pebbles and problems all solvable.

No greater love had I nor will I ever have!
Mothering my children and all to me.
An absolute gift from above,
And still with me in spirit, though departed.

Yes, there was a time when all that was true.
There will be a time we see each other once more.
When rainbows light the way to heaven,
That will be a time when I am again with you.

Grief

Your soul mate is ripped away!
True love, ground-hugging total grief … your love is gone.
Gravestone-kissing kind … you have nothing left to fight;
Your life a vacuum as you once knew it.
What was light, is dark … what was day, is night.

The why's crescendo in your ears,
Your gut, sour and long ago empty.
Energy-less you claw through every day,
A vague attempt to grasp reality,
But reality once known, has slipped away.

Minutes are hours … hours are years.
Every wakeful moment a continuum of hurt.
Time will never gain a foothold to ablate pain.
Your heart, mind and body … numb with loss.
There is no time left for you to try and sustain.

The dream of a painless shroud
Creeps into your brutalized mind.
Your life now saturated with sorrow;
You cannot escape the past!
But can you erase tomorrow?

Widower's Lament

Oh, beauteous one, lie by me!
Though heavens separate us,
Your soul permeates my being.
Your presence, a prescient feeling.

What evil force tore our connection?
Why life's torment?
Could another love have exceeded ours?
Alas! Human weaknesses.

Our seeds engendered three!
May kindness prevail,
And strength succeed,
Where else has failed.

Oh, soft lioness,
Your growl, like kisses,
Nurtured your loves.
The cold night to pass.

Redefine Love

How do you redefine love?
For over half my life,
Love has been and always will be
An association with someone special,
Someone who had always been close to me.

Someone who mothered my children,
Who I dined with and wined with,
Who I traveled with, near and far,
And yes, fought with and made up with,
And dreamed with under an evening star.

Love meant a union, friable yet strong,
Elastic and titanic, malleable and warm.
Differences, pliable and some implacable,
Dissentious, harbingers of the unexpected,
And yes, wounds unretractable

But the foundation was there,
Built on cohesion through time,
Built on mutual understanding and a goal.
Exacted over a life of trials and tribulation,
Not intended to be beached on waters-shoal.

And then, half of the union ripped away,
By a reveling intoxicant.
Body, nerves, shattered, the senses gone.
So sudden that it numbs the mind.
The ability to do right, preempted by doing wrong!

And with the passing, the meaning of love.
What possible relationship could warrant
The cocoon of that four-letter word?
Uttered, whispered in the idle of the night,
An expectation of comprehension? ... Absurd!

The rush to create, placate the pain of vacuum,
To construct a wall, to assuage, to deny;
Only to have to face the need
To meet reality head on ....
And redefine love.

Part 5
Umbra Solis
Ode to Life

I can feel the earth's rotation with the sinking of the setting sun?
Do you feel as I do that you are with this world as one?

Have you dived the rainbows of Bora Bora's coral reefs,
Or climbed the pinnacles of Machu Picchu's varied peaks?

Have you wafted along the tranquility of the upper Amazon's shores,
Or gazed below you from the Rockies' highest crags, when you could climb no more?

Have you spied for the spawning salmon in Alaska's far reaches?
Or bathed on Mexico's and Brazil's sandy beaches?

Have you floated France's wine-girded canals with fog drifting from dew-laden meadows,
Or trekked the winding trails ribboning through Italy's Cinque Terra shadows?

Have you seen the moon dance across the waters of a sylvan lake,
Or taken the wrong trail to a hidden heaven because of some mistake?

Have you trod through the blue and gold of the Tsars and all their opulence,
Or guided your sailing vessel at night by the stars, in blissful somnolence?

Have you looked with wonder on the aged Galapagos turtles crawling through history,
Or marveled with awe, on nature's natural mystery?

Have you paddled your canoe through Canada's Quetico in quest of the unknown,
Or gazed in total wonderment, upwards, and upwards to the tops of giant redwoods grown?

Have you mushed your sled dogs through frosted breath, on the Arctic Circle and north,
Or only imagined what's on the other side of Scotland's misty Firth of Forth?

Have you inched to the edge of Prekestolen to look down on Lysefjorden, two thousand feet below,
Or watched your bountiful orchards about to be harvested, and no more rows to hoe.

Have you started an arduous task and accepted success, ninety percent through,
Or that your orientation and direction were entirely wrong and you had to start anew?

Have you felt the crunch of Norway's deep pillowed snow, cross-country skiing in the early morn,
Or watched in a glade by a meandering stream, the marvel of an elk calf being born?

Have you dropped, repelling, from dizzying heights to a Belizean jungle cave, far below,
Or floated on rivers through miles of caverns where stalagmites slowly grow?

Have you completed a project upon which you had only dreamed,
Or realize that its complexity was far greater than it seemed?

Have you stood beside a four-thousand-year-old Bristle Cone Pine,
Or had the pleasure to satiate at the finest restaurants where you have dined?

Have you hacked a path through Columbia's thick jungle where there was no retreat,
Or stood atop windy, rainy, Haleakala, with a rainbow at your feet?

Have you blotted out man's cacophony as you slid along a Venetian waterway,
To mentally reincarnate to another time and another day?

Have you had a chance to relish the pleasure of imparting your prowess and acumen to others,
Or realized that finally you have achieved a laudatory place amongst your professional brothers?

Have you dreamed in Holland's Keukenhof Gardens amongst flowers in spectrum full,
Or in Vancouver's Butchart Gardens, where your heartstrings pull?

Have you said a silent prayer as you slowed to a quiet descent,
Or even contemplated if your chute cords had not become unbent

And have you crawled to the very top of the Santa Maria dome in Florence by the Arno,
Or reflected on what mortals will create in their quest for ascendancy, lest elsewhere they should go?

Have you felt the magnitude of tectonic shifting,
Or contemplated the dynamics of intercontinental plates drifting?

Have you stimulated your senses from Tuscany's Sangiovese grape growing on the vine,
Or wafted the nose of a Master Sommelier's billion-dollar wine?

Have you run in abject fear from The Bible Belt's tornadic wrath,
Or dodged at right angles to avoid its deadly path?

Have you donned your timber spurs and scaled the mighty northwest cedar to plus eighty feet,

Or driven cattle though wind and rain to the railhead to assuage the nation's crave for meat?

Have you "Manned the Rails" of a U.S. Navy carrier as she made her way into a foreign port,
Or watched the Statue of Liberty glide by, standing for freedom that others are trying to thwart?

Have you quietly rowed amongst playful manatees,
And watched closely, the bewhiskered hulk drink from your hose between his teeth?

Have you crawled through cactus and sage to sneak upon the wary Pronghorn,
To only be left on the shimmering-heated-plain - the fleet-one mocking you in scorn?

Have you watched twin fawns, wrapped in their placenta, waiting for mother's lingual caress,
A time-honored blessing to deliver them from duress?

Have you had a young great horned owl perch upon your hand and gaze at you with his big eyes,
Knowing full well that he would excel in the one being wise?

Have you felt the slam of a giant Bill on your rod and fought him to a standstill,
Then watched him gliding into the deep in departure, after releasing him to the ocean chill?

Have you ever tried to commune with the beauty of nature and all her vitalities,
From the vast forms of living to the myriad visual treasures; improbabilities are in fact realities?

Have you found yourself in guilt for some treacherous banality
And in contemplation of some psychotic expiation, considered finality?

Have you been resurrected from the depths of bipolarity
By timely minuscular tweaking of a cerebral biochemical modularity?

There are ups and downs, rounds and rounds to life's obvious bests
Delicate observation must be maintained for appreciation of the rest.

Have you visualized a Hump Back with her attending companion, giving birth to a young one;
Or enjoyed a Blue Morph, the tug of a Machaca, or plied the waters of Lake Arenal in the rising sun?

Have you tasted the dust from the Carrara quarries or smelled the sweetness of grapes on the vine,
Just part of the plethora of art, delectable cuisine, and never-ending Italy's exceptional wine?

Have you heard the cacophony of chimes, sailboat rigging while tethered to a dream,
Or wandered Oro de Montana's glorious trails, inhaling past, present and future, it would seem.

Perhaps you've been to Alaska, the bears, the whales, whose barnacled body you were able to touch.
Wilderness envelopes and endless skies greet tree tops where eagles clutch.

Have you seen the pinnacles of the Tetons from Idaho's grassy plain,
Grasping skyward as if more altitude to gain.
Or seen the kaleidoscopic lake-reflecting Fall glory,
Winter's precursor, a Bon Soir to a Summer story.

Or felt the mirrored images on Norway's placid lake
Questioning what's inverted, or your brain's mistake

Have you seen the Arctic's Aurora Borealis, fiery flares, caressing an ice-cold sky,
To accurately depict, an artist can only try.

Or a Rim-to-Rim one-day Grand Canyon hike,
On trails to nowhere, but everywhere, an incredible sight.

Or seen world-wide sunsets, today's closing image and a harbinger of a greeting to the other side;
While you while away the night and on moonbeams ride.

Have you smelled the Sulphur from Yellowstone's fire and brimstone, awaiting ignition,
Or thought about how it embellished the Ancient's superstition?

Have you been by river through a myriad locks, from Amsterdam to Budapest,
Living in the era of the Danube School of Vista Art, and all the rest?

The mountain solemnity to escape the metropolitan cacophonous roar,
Quietude, tranquility, sereneness, so your equanimity can soar.

Or perhaps opined on the illogicality of filial rejection,
And wondered if it was all due to genetic selection?

Have you witnessed the gray leviathans in the sky, vying for supremacy
Or contemplated power of nature's illumination, an act of natural normalcy.

Reflected on man's environmental ethic, or lack thereof, and a dying reef of coral,
Whose billions of creatures have succumbed – what sorrow!

Been to Africa, a sea of exotic creatures, terrestrial and all, an endless living motion
Bordered by the Neptunian Deep, a piscatorial living ocean.

Or perhaps the tenseness of 'Starboard Tack'! Sailing under pleasure but stress,
Awaiting the Committee Boat's starting gun for sailorly contest, on which to bless.

****

All this and much, much more has been my life.
Through unparalleled love, sickness and strife,
I've held the hands of loved-ones leaving;
And tried to console those who were grieving.

Four healthy children, and their children, lead me on,
To places unimagined and unseen vistas beyond.
Partners beyond all expectations,
Have accompanied me with love, encouragement and yes, their vexations.

The grim Reaper has dared look me in the eye,
But for some divine power, I was not supposed to die.
My future is not behind me until it's my time to capitulate,
Impossible and foolhardy to even try and calculate!

I've witnessed the juxtaposition of the happy against the sad,
What wondrous experiences I have had.
Yes! I feel I am, with this world, as one.
I have lived … "Umbra Solis" – in the shadow of the sun!

Aperçu

Poetry of love is in the hallways of my heart, doors that I've opened and closed during the wonderful moments gliding around reality, living vicariously and ignoring the verisimilitudes of life. A wonderful way to almost be in touch and yet avoid the incurring pitfalls. As life goes on, one indulges in shorter spans of fantasy and dwells more on what is now, what is probable, what is necessary to survive.

Poetry, if any at all, tends to wander around the chimerical, dancing with the make-believe, around what actually has happened, around the philosophical, around past present and future analysis of life. But even that tends to become mundane after a while as does life. Life is what life is, a continuing pathway from the beginning to the end, with hills and dales and abrupt ends and trails, but all the time getting a little shorter.

My poetry of love is around exalting experiences, around the almost impossible to believe and set in a rapturous setting that only the conjuring mind could conceive. It was fun writing while it lasted, but my mind is not capable of revisiting those periods. There is only so much space in my mind and heart for total twitter pated love and that disappears with age. Love takes on a new meaning, a mutual satisfaction and agreement of ideals and beliefs so that the minutes the days and the hours are filled with agreement and not dissonance.

It's easier that way. I can't call it love, I would instead call it a deep caring and sensitivity towards another.

Your breath, your touch, your movements – slight at times to totally convulsive; your eyes in the awakening light of day, the shadows across your face where a thousand angels have danced, your laughter, your grace, your ability to glide from room to room without taking a step. All of these and a plethora of more will always be indelibly in my mind.

Chapter II

Ranch and Range
Poetic Musing

"V Rock"

"V Rock", "San Juan Mountains as sketched by Mary Wood from our front porch, Pagosa Springs, CO"

Preamble

I was born in Sheridan, Wyoming and spent my younger years on my parent's dude/cattle ranch, Rapid Creek, on the eastern Bighorns. I worked on my father's ranch near Gillette, and others, and lived all over the United States. I never cease to be inspired by the West's wide-open spaces, the grandeur of the views, the magnificence of the mountains, the plethora of rushing mountain streams filled with the elusive trout, the lore of the west and the honesty, strength of character and sense of humor in those living there. And in particular, the special places where I continue to visit that keep the wonderful memories alive. The West is open, broadminded, beckoning, and beautiful!

There is unanimity of opinion that no country in America is more lovely than the eastern slope of the Bighorn Mountains.

I call it home!

My writings can be loose, meander and are not age specific. You will find a little humor, pathos, philosophy, reflection and whimsy. Ribaldry is also part of my demeanor and seeks its own window from time to time. Poetry has a broad palette.

These few musings, vignettes and narrations are a small indication of my unwavering respect for those still here and the memories of those gone, the Westerners upon which the West was built.

"feel ye and thou shall understand"

The Procrastinator

Do you remember when you were a wee, wee tot
And all that kind of rot?
Well, now you are older and wiser
And somewhat of an analyzer.

You spy that little gray house across the yard,
Across a barren wasteland and ground, Oh so hard!
Across drifted fields of snow
And inside that "One-Holer" it's forty below.

There is a rope from the house to out yonder,
Lest in a blizzard you should wander.
Or you should slip and fall in the mud and rain,
And toward the home you should lose your aim.

That old dry door swings and creaks on rusted hinge,
And the mere thought of that trip makes you cringe.
The wind drives the cold right through the cracks
And that cold snow-covered seat will run a knife right up your back.

It's bad enough just to take the chance
But then you have to drop your pants.
Really, there must be a better way.
I know, I'll just wait another day.

Good Morning

Have you ever seen the rising sun through a drop of rain in the
morning light,
The awakening of the dawn
from the previous night?

Have you watched as the mountains take shape,
A mold coming into view,
Or watched the gentle movement
Of the Spider's web, covered with silvery dew?

Have you heard the early heralding twitter,
The stories that are told
By the restless young, their parents,
The feathered, young and old?

Have you seen an ant, one side in light,
The other in shade,
As he ascends a wavering stem,
An aphid for a meal to be made?

Have you watched a mountain stream
Come to life,
The critters and creatures, twigs and things,
Singing like a distant fife?

Have you realized that the tumbling
Always caries on,
Never stops,
Breathing a message to a darkness gone?

Have you listened to the utter complete silence
Of an early morn,
The newness and sweetness
Of a day reborn?

Have you felt the gentle touch of the breeze
Upon your face,
And realized ...
This is God's holy place?

Call of The Mountains

The mountains call,
But that's not all,
There's a beckoning force within.
The dark and the green,
Or the white serene,
Away from the city's din.

The falling waters,
Playful otters,
The pull is undeniable.
Reflective pools,
Nature's tools,
A character, always pliable.

Breath the life of an Evergreen tree,
Feel, what the eagles see,
Absorb - what creation brings!
The path ahead,
Will clear your head.
Listen! - To how the silence sings.

Black clouds hover,
Rainy shrouds cover,
Lingering mists remain.
From the storm's shadow, the peeking sun,
The rainbow's hues where the colors run,
And all in your domain.

The wind may moan,
The standing giants groan,
Or a zephyr soft upon your face.
Utter stillness may prevail,
As you trek a dusty trail,
An answer to life's daily race.

Nature's dynamic folds,
See how it molds
Your life to intertwine.
A treasure stable,
A gift-laden table,
The mountains are yours to find.

Few Left

The moonlight is astraddle
A cold and empty saddle,
Somewhere out on the range.
A cowboy got throw'd,
But nobody know'd;
And that's not really strange.

For a cowboy's life is alone;
His bedroll is his home,
As he wanders the mountains and plains.
His best friend, of course,
Is his trusted horse;
And he's happiest, hand holding the reins.

He's got the world at night,
The stars an awesome sight,
Until the sun comes up over the rim.
A little old fire,
Till that orb creeps higher,
And contentment is coffee to the brim.

It's a life he's chosen,
Either too hot or half frozen,
All in the work of a day.
He'll get the right count,
Until his dismount,
And wouldn't have it any other way.

Now of the real cowboy, there's just a few.
The ranch has changed, it's entirely new.
Sort of cowboys, new ones might be,
It's their way of life;
Some even have a wife!
But they'll never know - riding free.

Lightning Strikes

Cowboys are tough!
There's no doubt about that.
But match against the flash?
It'll cut you no slack.

They're a lightning rod,
Sitting straight in their saddle.
Horse and man astraddle,
Wet to the ground.

A fate temptation,
Sentencing from the sky …
They just keep herding
And never ask why!

I've heard of quite a few,
But only two that I really knew;
Both good friends,
One lived, ... the other died.

Elusive One

What timid shadow is that,
stirring on the gravely interface
of sublimity and reality?
That elongate dream of detached amusement,
That flash of color,
racing between sun and rock,
That soft apparition,
floating from cloud to cloud?

What chance to glimpse
God's perfect shape,
The plexus of geometric form,
Yet independent attitude
mirror-imaging the soul.
The nidus of serendipitous dream,
Yours is the heaven that exists
In the cool rush of the mountain stream.

Easy Drive

It was about seventy some years ago;
Gillette, where things moved pretty slow.
The summer had been dry,
The feed good,
The last thing we wanted now was rain.
You'd leave weight-gain on the plain.

But move 'em slow we did.
Pretty much as the trail boss bid.
Just shy of three thousand,
Not a big bunch,
But enough to tie up a loose end;
And many a mile of fence to mend.

Heard the boss's wife would be at the railhead.
Bit strange, usually the big man, himself instead.
Heard she had a head for figures,
Nary missed a critter.
Few clouds about,
But we're only a day out.

Camped on the Powder that night,
Stars an awesome sight.
Towards morn, a bit breezy,
Something's probably moving in.
Coffee and vittles with day-break.
Shake 'em loose – another day to make.

Got a bit gray
As we moved along the way.
Still no bother,
We're almost there.
Five mile or so
Is all we have to go.

Come night, we crowded all at last.
Summer of grazing is now past.
The boss will winter a few hundred or more,
Limited hay and the winter will be hard.
A few days on the trail
From the ranch to the rail.

It's their last ride
And our pride.
Each year the same,
But each year a little different.
It is a job well done,
Some pain, some fun.

Rain the next day, the dam broke.
But we had 'em there – a lucky stroke,
Up the chutes – into the cars;
The boss's wife keeping tally.
No shrinkage this time,
They come through just fine.

Probably the best of all.
So now we're through,
Back to the ranch we go.
Buy in the spring,
Sell in the fall.
It's a beautiful way of life.

Elegy to Curly
Stampede

Just Curly and me on that fateful night,
Holding herd with the other three.
Together, we'd seen 'bout every sight,
But know'd 'bout some we feared to see.

Air quiet and dry … too dry.
Your breath crackles.
You can feel the tension in the sky,
On edge, all your hackles.

Gotta keep em bedded.
Horizon's all alight.
If they git up … a move that's dreaded.
"Sing to em … don't let em fright!"

From here to yon and back agin,
There's Almighty hell up there.
Stay as sheet fire! … Then no cracking din.
"We're OK, we'll make it fair."

But cut it lose,
And there's no turning back.
Ten thousand wild eyes … a hangman's noose,
And in the rope, there'll be no slack.

You can cut the air,
Smell that 'lectric smell,
Faint, but enough to curl your hair.
Jump em up … you're on the way to hell!

The heavens blacken,
The streaks more intense.
If only this weather would slacken,
It just don't make no sense.

K R R A A A C K K

and the ground begins to rumble!

There's movement now.
"Oh Lord! Horse don't stumble!
Just give me strength and show me how."

Five thousand stampede as one,
A sea of wild-eyed terror.
The lightning strikes … thunder a gun !
Evil on the hoof … death-bearer!

Curly, me, Pard, Luke and Jake,
Got to turn em, got to try.
Fear and bellerin', it's our damned fate …
Driven by fire in the sky.

"Wheel 'em," Curly cries.
"Up the hill!"
And his horse goes down … and Curly dies.
And nothing, nothing, is still.

The ground is boiling.
You react, that's all.
The sky is roiling;
Horse, don't fall !

Along at a terrible pace !
The lead is turning,
And you gain in the race.
Your world is churning.

Heaven's anger hath been wrought,
It's over now; you've won, or have you?
This is the type of work you've sought,
But have you the courage to see it through?

How long? ... Who's left?
What's the point ... what's the cost?
Pick up the pieces ... a short rest.
And a prayer for a good man gone;   Curly lost!

Night Stop

The moonlight is fragmented into bits of light
As through the trees it drifts,
Falling on pine needles and night critters,
Sorting shadows, it slowly sifts.

The lowing is silent, the heard is bedded;
The cavy quiet, the hands at rest.
Morning, too soon will come,
Old coals, a lingering fragrance at best.

An owl hoots a mournful call,
To a mate perhaps, a moonbeam riding.
Their time is short, a darkened moment,
With day, into hiding.

A cattleman's dream is not interrupted
By thoughts not akin to his life;
For each day is a cycle of work and toil,
And each night ... re-whetting the knife.

139

That sharp well-honed edge
That keeps the mind in tune
With what lays ahead on the morrow,
Lest it all be over too soon.

Lochinvar

Let me tell you a story 'bout a friend of mine;
No, it doesn't begin with ,"Once upon a time."
This is about a man with a very special talent;
The envy of many others ... Oh, he was so gallant!

Why, he could rope a rainbow, that's what he could do.
He brought to the table more than me and you.
The young ladies would just swoon in his way,
Their hearts were just gone before he'd even stay.

He'd ride out of town on his trusty steed,
Having committed the most unforgivable deed.
Why, just by riding by, he'd collect three or four,
Without even knocking on any one's door.

Oh Yeah! His reputation preceded his coming.
The birds a flutter and the bees just a humming.
Even the wind would die down in anticipation,
And the women sensed it - without hesitation.

No one cared whether he was six foot four or five feet two;
How he was dressed, nobody knew.
It was not what he said or how he sang his song,
It was partly because he never tarried too long.

He courted with great and utmost care,
Never enabling another man to dare
To follow in his mannerly ways;
And always leaving behind ... the sun's warming rays.

His company was relished by all who knew
That talk was only talk … but it's what he could do.
Young ladies of the west just want you to know,
That you just have to learn … to rope a rainbow!

I Guess, Kinda, Maybe

I guess, kinda, maybe,
I looked into her eyes.
"The two of us could be we",
I said much to her surprise.

Thus, our lives began.
She had a love for all,
More than I could understand,
All creatures, great and small.

And to our lives there crept
Small young ones wee;
Such joy, we often wept,
A glorious sight to see.

And then those little ones,
To grownups they grew,
And had daughters and sons;
And like chaff before the wind, they blew.

And now we sit and dream awhile,
And watch the days slip by.
We lived and loved in style,
And now listen to the evening breezes sigh.

They tell a sweet tale
Of two souls grown to one,
Of two lives, a union, n'ere to fail,
Of wild flowers beneath the sun.

Lives, like flowers,
May blossom and flourish;
Yet they too must fade 'round the bowers,
Memorable fragrances, for others to nourish.

"Well, I guess, kinda, maybe,"
I looked into her eyes;
"The night is near, you can see,
To bed! – for tomorrow we must rise."

Past Tense

I used to get a thrill
To see an elk come over the hill,
To see a suckling calf in the valley below,
To hear the turkey call just before night,
To see the shadows, fade in evening light.

But the cogs don't mesh now,
Nor do I really know how
To make them synchronous again.
There is simply no more flow,
Like the drying stream below.

Like the candle flame,
The inevitable end to the same.
A flicker, a flare and then it's gone.
A fleeting moment of inner peace,
It's perfidy to have it cease.

Pebbles

"Why do you sit there,
Watching the ripples as they run?
They disappear, Old Man,
Even that, you can understand."

> *"So true my son,*
> *But linger, to absorb full value.*
> *'Tis the subtle essence,*
> *That should dominate their presence."*

"But why not cast another pebble
And look for something new?
Quick! Before they diminish.
Don't miss watching before they finish."

> *"Ah! But you see,*
> *There lies the dilemma.*
> *Want you a little of a lot,*
> *Or a lot of a little ... and relish the plot?"*

"Your bucket of pebbles,
Each one an experience;
All you must cast
Lest you fail to throw the last!"

> *"No, I was given a charge,*
> *As were you.*
> *With the pebbles, be not abrupt;*
> *It is to savor each, not use them up."*

"Then if you should die
With half a bucket left;
Did you not squander opportunity,
Just to gain scrutiny?"

"Is a rose observed
All at once,
Or by petal, fragrance and blush?
Hurry not! There is no rush."

"You mean quality over quantity,
Is that your indication?
The casting should last,
Lest the experience be lost to the past?"

"Exactly! The passage of life,
We must run.
Use your pebbles wisely,
Lest you miss the fun!"

Morning

The saddle settles gently on a tense back,
Talking to you on a frosty morn,
Creaking as leather loosens up.
Warm smells emanate from the barn.

Rooster hailing the day outback;
Breath, signally temperature differences;
Lazy cats now animated fur-balls;
Your dog now fully awake.

Distant critters lowing on the bottoms,
Feathered friends greeting the rising sun;
Yeah! It's good to be alive.
Mount up for wranglin' chores!

Eastern Law – Western Judge

"His minacious loquacity
Inhibits his capacity
For ebullient eloquence.
His delivery predilection
And verbal deception,
Stifles any credence."

"His obtestation,
A heinous supplication,
To veil Your Honor's intelligence.
A derisive obfuscation,
Builds on prevarication,
Questing the jury's benevolence."

"What you really have here,
And I want to make this quite clear,
Over other counsel's objection,
Is an attempt to elude
Verisimilitude;
And divert the court's direction."

"So, Your Honor, I implore,
As, confabulation I abhor,
Please make this hearing more formal.
And do not sustain
His ridiculous acclaim.
Make his aberrations more normal."

"But I must really address
His chance for success
And request his abjuration.
I 'd further be remiss
If I didn't seek to dismiss
The utterly ridiculous allegation."

145

To all this the judge replied,
As over his specs he spied,
"You speak with good intent.
But your logorrheic rhyme
Takes up my time.
Now **shut-up** ... or
I'll hold you in contempt!"

Room Service

Gaudy-Bawdy was a sweet girl,
Perhaps not too clean,
But she meant well,
When she sought the job
At the Hotel Doreen.

Now that hotel was right on the trail
Of the drovers,
As they moved the cattle through the dust.
And like as such
It was frequented much by those lusty men
Who knew what they wanted,
And had money to pay
For whatever play
Suited their manly physique.

It was one stormy night
When a ranny named Ben climbed into bed
In that spirited house,
All decorated with chartreuse and red.

He was down to his last buck
And was too tuckered to pee,
When somewhere down the hall,
Gaudy-Bawdy was prowling;
As could be told
By her raucous and fervent plea.

"Room Service" she would hack,
"Coffee, tea or me."
My, how sweet Gaudy-Bawdy had changed,
Her job title too,
For now, tips were made on her back.

What happened next?
Nobody really knows,
But it must have gone something like this:

Old Ben was a man with insatiable pride,
And unwilling to admit defeat,
While Gaudy-Bawdy wanted money;
And in no way would she retreat.

Well they did it all night
And into the next day,
And some say missed six meals.

But that's not strange,
Out on the range,
Where a man is measured by his *poke.* *
And if fail he must
In the quest of lust,
Then he must hang by the end of a rope.

And so it was the following morn,
That they found him battered and torn,
Hanging from the balcony stay.
And who was seen boarding the stage,
Gaudy-Bawdy counting her pay.

Let this be a warning to you young studs,
To lock your doors
And forget the whores,
Lest you wind up scared and nervous;
By someone knocking in the middle of night;
And bellowing out,   **"ROOM SERVICE".**

A small satchel that where a cowboy carried all his belongings.

The Hike

A thousand sets
Of a hundred reps,
Your weight plus a pack.
You make the accent
To your heart's content,
And then you have to go back.

But at the end of the fun,
The day's not done;
For memories linger there.
Wildflowers in glorious hue,
Sky of an incredible blue,
And a return? Your fervent prayer!

Mountain Stream

Could there be anything greater
Than to be alone with your creator,
Fishing on a mountain stream?
Anyone of us know, that's the ultimate,
A nature lover's dream.

The trout in hiding,
Against the current, gently gliding,
Knowing that they are the axis of the world,
Not some man's scientific folly;
As she lies beneath the waters softly swirled.

A morsel drifts by
And in the twinkle of an eye,
That tidbit is devoured.
By divine intervention,
That disappearing image is now empowered.

To wander from rock to rock
To play with its shadow as if to mock
It's double to try and stay abreast,
Or seeking quietude,
It's under an embankment to rest.

You're motionless, gazing at the wonder,
Not daring to break the peace asunder.
Your fishing is complete!
Your day is done, the fly not wetted -- dry.
Every desire, replete.

Night Stillness

All is still, or is it?
Night critters!
They are there,
Elk, deer, coyote,
Maybe even a bear.

The owl is about - can't see him.
He counts on that.
Magic in the air.
A feast here,
A tidbit there.

A mouse's eyes, big and alert,
He tries to see the world.
The rabbit hopping,
Grassy blade to succulent morsel,
Its hunger never stopping.

The dark, alive, movement everywhere.
Day creatures hiding,
Their time will come.
Let the night slide away,
With the coming of the sun.

Days come and the days go.
The light will fade,
And night will step in between.
Creatures in light,
At night, are seldom seen.

And at night,
When only the stars are watching,
Critters come out and make no noise.
They're mostly silent,
Enjoying nocturnal joys.

So, listen and imagine
What's out there -- moving about.
It may seem to you
That all is hushed.
Night is not for you to view.

Ode to The Hunter

"Me, a hunter", or so I say.
"I can talk real big 'bout the one that got away,
Or how the big bull got stole out of my truck,
Or how my rifle misfired on that Boon and Crocket buck.

"Or in the Rockies, when that blizzard made us leave our game.
That was in ought-three, one died and two came out lame.
I don't have trophies on the wall,
But I can tell you-all 'bout them -- as I stand big and tall.

"Now my belly may be big,
And I may swill beer and stink like a pig,
But I am one of the hearty breed.
To the best racks in the country – I'll take the lead.

"So, to all your hunter friends, you just go and tell
How Big Man can guide them out of hell,
Out of the canyons of no return,
And through trees so thick, a fire can't burn.

"Of stories so grand, their minds I will bend,
They'll believe they've been there and others they will send.
Tales of The Big Man and just what a hunter is he,
For I have seen Satan's wrath – and a trophy man is me."

Imagine

Imagine, if you will,
Just where you are,
Under heaven
And beneath every bright star.

You have ridden the dusty trail,
Crossed a million streams,
Loped across a park or two,
To arrive at the place of your dreams.

Your day is done, you lie on your bedroll.
The pines reach the sky.
The wind whispers sweet nothings,
As the jewels in the sky drift slowly by.

There! -- The bright one,
Part of Orion you think.
It was above the bough,
Now rotation makes it sink

The fragrance of the fire,
Ebbing to its final glow,
The wisps of smoke,
Tantalizing you to just let go.

Dream your dreams,
Because you are there --
At lake-side high in the mountains,
The wild ones lair.

The home of the peaceful,
The land of grace.
The elegance,
Putting everything in place.

Sage Advice

"So, you want to be a cowboy,"
Said Grandpa to Little Boots!
"It's different now
Than when I was reared.

We needed a hay-stacker
and a good Percheron team.
Weren't no bailers back then,
On which to lean.

Bailers were kind a new,
Bound 'em with wire
Not string.
Now, Bailers for hire.

Had to be handy with a forge,
Know a 'single jack'
From a mawl,
And have a strong back.

Now-a-days, call a Farrier.
Be your own vet,
Pull you own calf.
Now, Vet's best bet.

Pitch a fork full of hay,
Don't over-do the grain.
Now, formula balanced-out feed.
Convoluted pain!

Post holes dug by hand,
Not many in a day.
Now hydraulic diggers,
Modern machinery ... it's a new way.

Chaps were functional,
Not dude-fancy ... fake pride.
Used to keep a thorny-thicket
Off your hide.

You'd ride hell-n-gone
Just to see if a critter was there.
Now you have a cell phone
And a drone that'll look anywhere.

You made a little money,
Besides jack-pot roping.
Enough for a Saturday night,
To get one, you'd be hoping.

There's a lot, didn't have back then,
But we didn't hurt for none.
We rolled out at sun-up
And did what needed to be done.

Sometimes you're so dang hot
You'd swear your innards going to boil.
Then there is winter,
And a different kind of toil.

Naw, Little Boots,
It's different now.
Fella has to know more,
Than just a heifer from a cow.

But if'n that's what you want,
There's nary a better life.
Beats the hell out of city livin',
And that cramped up kind a strife.

You're pretty handy
With your cayuse,
But there's more than just that,
…… If you're to be of any use.

You'll have to git some schoolin'
If'n your going to succeed.
Learn the new ways,
But keep the old ethic … indeed.

If you are on the outside, you're lookin' in;
If you're on the inside, your lookin' out.
The grass is always just a little greener,
Seems that's what cow-boyin' is all about.

There are some things you just can't describe,
An early morn wrangle is still great.
Nature's yours to have-n- hold,
Make no mistake!

The cowboy's domain
Is his alone.
The ranch is his life,
And the range, his home."

Query

Inspired by Vladimir Nabokov's short story, "Wood Sprite", 1929.

"Allow me to introduce myself," say I.
"Your ranch, my first residence,
Whence on my birth, I arrived;
Seventy-five years since, I've survived.

Memories from too early to remember;
Toddling, riding, hide and seek, fishing,
All along the infamous Rapid Creek.
A mark upon my soul – a kiss upon my cheek!

A pathway amongst gurgling laughter,
Shadows chasing shadows,
Tree cotton dancing to waters below,
Where swirling pools ebb and flow.

A movement or a flash,
Imagination it would seem,
But wait, … there, … more than one,
An aquatic zephyr in the sun.

Unconsciously exalted, minute by minute,
Again, and again, hour by hour.
What utter complete bliss!
Not a breeze-wafted particle to miss.

A period of harmony with the world!
No mystery could possibly hide
The rapturous rustling
Of joyous, playful tussling.

Heaven's overture to a child's life.
Protected, caressed and blessed
By nature's embracing hands,
I, in the Bighorn's gentle lands.

How could I conceivably leave?
What force could rip apart?
But alas, life moves on!
And I, at age nine, was gone.

Gone, but never forgotten!
And now I do beseech
A re-visitation to walk the ways,
An invitation to my childhood days

Amongst the friendly meandering reverie,
The memories now dreamed of.
I live to seek,
My youthful days back on Rapid Creek."

Rapid Creek Ranch, author's first home

Excursus

Just a Thought

And I watched the man. I watched as he came through the creaking front door, in from out of the cold, dog-weary from feeding and all the other work that goes with being a rancher. You could see that he was chilled through and through.

He didn't know I was watching him, had no idea I was even there. He stoked up the fire, warmed himself a bit and then shed his coat, stretched a little and settled into a big, very old, easy chair. I figured he would stay there awhile; but I was wrong, 'cause he was restless. He'd squirm this-a-way and that-a-way – generally seemed unsettled; kind of like something was bothering him. And it was, 'cept he didn't really know what it was.

Deep down within the man there was something gnawing at his subconscious. There was a spark that was gently being fanned into a flame. His subconscious, was in its inevitable way, signaling his conscious self to do something; but his awake self was still too bottled up with the day's thoughts to register. It was only after a while that he really began to understand what was happening.

Just a glow of an idea. No, he wouldn't bother with it. Yet the idea persisted. And he thought, 'Why not'? His head nodded a little; and for a minute I thought he was apt to take a nap, but then as I looked, I could see that his head bobbed rhythmically, kind of like trying to carry a tune without saying anything. You could see now that his conscious self was registering. The idea had broken through. Yes, he did want to hear a little music and most of all to be a part of it – might make him relax a little.

But he still sat there thinking, this time, on the rather limited repertoire of songs that he knew. Nope, he wasn't much of a singer, but he could play the mandolin – not half badly. And he thought about what he might play.

He slowly got up, stretched his long legs, which were already starting to stiffen up. There in the far corner of the room, behind a table and half wedged behind the sofa, was the old mandolin he'd been given by his dad. It had belonged to his grandfather and was a memento he'd always cherished. Oh, he'd cared for it – thought about it when he was working sometimes – made the chores easier. Thought about what he'd like to be able to play and just what he was able to play, there was quite a difference, and he pondered over that too.

Actually, he did a lot of thinking when it came to music so it was no surprise to see him treat that case with the mandolin in it like a week-old baby. He opened it ever so gently and cocked his head as he admired the fade-light reflection playing games on the high-sheen finish he so carefully made sure was there each time he put the instrument away. Now he settled back in his chair, having put the case aside after gently closing it.

The mandolin sat in his lap for a few moments as he sought to gather his thoughts, his musical thoughts; for the one thing he wanted to avoid was a discordant sound. What had to come to the ear would be soft and sweet; and the best way to assure that, was to think carefully about what strings to touch, in what order and how many at a time, singly or as a chord, gently or a more generous – strum. And he had to make sure the instrument was in tune, was ready to come alive and give back in return what he so dearly wanted to hear. If it was to be as he wanted it to be, it had to be a give and take affair. A proper warming-up – an exchange of sweetness. No way could he just grab the mandolin, kick the case aside and pick at just any old string without cause and expect it to respond.

Now he held her and ever so gently, having formulated exactly what he wanted to play in his mind, conveyed his thoughts to the strings. And you know what? The melody filled the room and warmed it. It lifted his sagging spirit. He and the mandolin were as one. They were communicating. And the amazing thing is that he didn't even realize all the myriad thought processes that went into the generation of those lovely tunes that emanated from that instrument; for they were in synchrony, they were in harmony.

I let him play until he was finished and fed himself and then and only then when he was seated back in his favorite chair, did I beat a little tune on his brain and ask him in a way that only his subconscious could comprehend:

"Hey Pal, you thought of ever treating your lady like you do that mandolin? You ever thought that maybe, just maybe, she might be a tad more responsive and sympathetic to your whims if you showed her as much tenderness? You can't just reach over and jerk her chain or pluck her chord or whatever you call it and expect a pretty tune!

Think! You have to be gentle! Open her case carefully, tune her, communicate with her, play her softly, not rushing to crescendo. Put her away slowly, having made sure she is comfortable. Where's that sheen, that sparkle in her eye? Let her slumber in peace, knowing that you have taken the best care of her that you can. You want her to be responsive next time, to arise to your music making? Then Pal, give her the same attention and thought that you do to that mandolin. You do that and I assure you, there will be sweet music."

Treat each other as a fine musical instrument and beautiful sounds will be forthcoming and everlasting.

"He", has no defining gender.
For where would he be
Without **she**,
As the gentle mender?

CHAPTER III

My World

Emotivity of Bipolarity

Preamble

Unmanageable and disturbing frequent vacillations between elation and suicidal ideation necessitated psychiatric intervention, the result being a medical diagnosis of cycling bipolarity. That was in the 1980's. Etiology? ... presumed to be a biochemical imbalance that could be ameliorated by pharmaceuticals. *Archaic thinking*!

That, I don't ridicule! However, there is another very significant element, situational. And what weight does that carry? That is categorically unquantifiable! It is also something that is mutable within the individual and can be internally processed over time, to varying degrees of success.

I am a pharmacophobic; if conceivably possible, I will avoid medications. I have survived, but not without a lot of mental gyrations. The good certainly outweighs the bad, the latter having almost succeeded on two occasions, once as an adolescent and once in my fifties.

What has been derived? Poetic expressions written over time, reflecting the darker side as well as the lighter side, have given me a release and something to mull over retrospectively.

Depression, elation, awe and anger, are some of the emotive feelings that permeate the poetry. Laced with lyric and narrative, encompassing pathos, philosophical, humor, and ribaldry, and love of life, they take you through years of mental frustrations over a perplexing dichotomy of emotions. I offer them up to the reader, randomized, just as life presents itself, for your interpretation.

My writing is totally subjective .... If I feel it, I put it down; I don't ponder how I should express myself. I lay it all on the table, as it comes from my heart at that moment of time ... like it or not.

Thank you to those, family and friends, who have endured my mood swings with patience and love, especially late wife Unni and my dear wife, Mary.

"feel ye and thou shall understand"

My Intent

It matters not how long the day,
I work for love, not pay.
A smile or two will do,
And your realization that I love you.

Another moment ne'er to repeat,
Time does not retreat.
Only memories depict history,
The future remains a mystery.

How long to see stamina fade,
Dimming light creating shade?
Horizons rearing clear,
Must counteract that fear.

An inevitability, nature's way,
Mere mortals have naught to say.
Live, love as best you can,
Leave a legacy as a gentle man.

My omissions, only human.
Malice intent, not proven.
Days that I will always rue
Until my time runs out.

Joy Killers

When all around you try to give advice
On what you should aspire to - that just might suffice
To satiate your rambling desires;
And to others create something that one admires.
To those and others who assume to be anthropomorphistic,
You are not imbued with the prescience of a mystic.

An idea cerebrally conjured is a product of intellectuality,
Not necessarily a departure from normality,
And thus, worthy of consideration;
Not a ridiculous unobtainable aberration.
Let not then, those with presumptions of perspicacity,
Become joy-killers, due to limited sagacity.

Twenty-four Hours

The hand spins twice!
What surcease is there to satiate
The constant gnawing of hunger
Of emotional deprivation?

That ravenous contempt
That continuously fills the void
Of sensible cerebration,
Stimulating self-extermination.

Why the exposure to perfection,
Only to be rotted by the putrefaction
Of greater ideologies
That should stand by ideation alone?

Is it all an abysmal impossible dream,
Not to be awakened from?
A sick and unsound mind coursing life
In a circuitous maelstrom of depression!

Where is the end – or is there none?
Where is the light – and then some?
Where is life – without mental strife?

Age-old Dilemma

I'm giving in you see.
Not strong enough to run the race.
Mind and body separate
Great dreams from reality.

Doubts accumulate,
Smothering the verve, the zest.
Acceptance – difficult.
Declining at an alarming rate.

Is it time to just smell the roses,
And let others do what you used to?
Is it time to live on memories,
And stop trying to create?

Age is inevitable!
It's just unpleasant!
Why can't inner peace,
Be more tangible?

Duplicity

Duplicity, felicity,
Go hand in hand.
A woman's emotion,
On demand.

To play the role,
To weave the web
Where the common man,
Should fear to tread.

And should there he goes,
Then it would be no surprise,
That with pain and heartache,
He would meet his demise.

Self-Analysis

Don't try to figure me out!
I've survived for 82 years –
Being an enigma to myself.

To me, I'm not perplexing!
Occasionally unpredictable,
Perhaps a tad over-vexing.

Change is not incumbent upon me!
Impossibility it would seem -
I'd rather be myself than thee.

So, let me linger in my twilight years,
Savor the moments given throughout,
Never to stress nor be reduced to tears.

My plea is a simple supplication!
Let me live as I have been able to do.
Enjoying each serendipitous revelation.

Why?

What frailties encroach upon me
As older I get!
How my horizons diminish,
My emotions dwindle.

No excitement swells my day,
No great urges to arise and do.
No elations over things well done.
No accomplishments to dwell on.

Is this what age is about,
An encroaching veil of hopelessness?
A continual darkening of highlights,
Till blackness, curtains fall?

No acknowledgements for deeds past,
No recognition for years of toil,
No respect except from a few peers,
Those that are still living and near.

You learned in the past
To avoid pain and strife.
Then what the hell is the point
Of continuing your life?

Where Did It Go

Bipolarity decreases the probability of creative imagination,
Or so it would seem, given the obscurity of poetic machination.
So, what to squelch such cerebral disturbances -
The stagnation of emotive emotions.

Reasoning

Do you ever do anything for absolutely no reason at all,
Like getting out of bed just to find your feet in the hall?
Do we really have to have a reason just to do something?
Does a bird actually contemplate, before he takes wing?
Maybe think, before you jump, lest you tumble and fall.

Fate, Your Shadow

Gann wrote, "Fate Is the Hunter".
I write, "Fate Is Your Shadow".

Fate is your shadow,
Waiting to destroy or embellish.
Dreams of grandeur,
Fantasies to relish.

Fate, though fickle
Has her own line of reason;
A helping hand,
Or act of treason.

Is fate destiny,
Or destiny fate?
In the eyes of the beholder,
It's what you make.

Perhaps like the current,
It goes with the flow.
The ebb and turning,
Direction so slow.

A signal to transmit?
Inevitable conclusion?
Kismet be damned!
Unwanted obtrusion.

Old plans to amend,
If fate is to be thwarted,
Not be resurrected again;
Then plans must be aborted.

No one knows what tomorrow will bring.
Check your shadow tonight;
And if you can read it,
You'll be alright.

The chances are
That as each idea is born,
It will leave someone unhappy,
Someone forlorn.

Such is the balance,
Tween earth and sky.
Rest ye not,
Nor dare ye ask why!

How?

How can you know where you are going,
When you don't know where you've been?
How can you preach sobriety,
When you live in a bottle of Gin?

How can there be meaning to life,
When all around you are dead?
Perplexities go unanswered,
When there are cavitations in your head.

Direction comes from within,
Stoked by memories coherent.
Illumination of way,
By cerebrations adherent.

Preparation

It's not really clear
If the end is near,
But signs would make me believe
That I'd better gather my stuff;
Blithe attendance is not enough,
If other's concerns I'm to relieve.

For to end my path
And appease God's wrath,
I'd better get my affairs in line.
Organized chaos is acceptable,
If belongings are not collectable;
But a few things I consider quite fine.

Its papers here and papers there
And corruption spread everywhere.
What choice then have I,
But to jettison most;
And relieve my Host
Of having to ask, "Why?"

At Eighty

I'm tired of pretending
That I'm a young man.
I'm tired of pretending
That I know I can.
I'm tired of make believe,
That emotions are on my sleeve.
Can't you see,
They are deep within the heart of me.

Why can't I just rest,
And not jump to every whim
That others might suggest?
My horizons are dim!
Must cease my pushing ahead!
Why can't I stop, rest instead?
I don't want too soon to die,
I just want, that I don't always have to try.

I care little which team really won,
Or what the score.
Just a home run,
Or two points for more?
Eagles and Hat Tricks,
Double-doubles and Lacrosse sticks,
Or whipped in a Love-set;
Matters little - millions they'll get.

I feel I am tired,
And weary to the bone
Trying to live the hour – already expired.
But for why, I've not toiled alone!
If only others could see,
Concern is for my family.
Through memories they must gain,
Avoidance of pitfalls, and contentment attain.

I'm tired of pretending
That I am who people think I am.
And I must learn to relax in serenity.

Over

There is little joy on the horizon,
All the day's work, done.
What's the point of living?
Life's race - been run.

My Mary

My Mary is financially taken care of,
But her emotional needs will be great.
If my family has a grain of salt in them,
They will step up to the plate.

Her love and respect have been earned!
Only time will tell
If my children will meet her in heaven;
Or end up in hell.

Passages

Drs. Daniel R. Stough and Nate Bradley, out of Oklahoma City, put my broken neck back together after a fatal car accident in 1997 with a drunk driver, robbing me of my wife of thirty-five years. In 2002, Dan was diagnosed with a melanoma, which subsequently metastasized to his brain. He is now deceased! Doctor Bradley lives in California.

I am here and happily remarried to my lovely Mary who put Humpty-Dumpty back together again!

As others pass through our lives,
So, we through others.
Simplistic, it would seem,
Just sisters and brothers.
A convenient balance of friendships.

No such thing as perfect balance,
Just as no such thing as total perfection.
Physics won't allow, all is in constant motion,
From minuscular molecular modalities,
To stratospheric and tectonic totalities.

One friend arrives, one friend leaves.
Like autumnal changes ... I think not.
What the size, what the import,
What the moral fiber, what the weight?
Not who we are, but what we create!

Friendship or passing acquaintance,
Don't try to equate!
One more important than the other,
A brief encounter with one who gives you life,
Versus a confident you have through glee and strife?

We are who we are,
Leaving tracks that only He knows,
Trekking the trails confronting us,
Filling our footprints with feats.

You, ... creator of feats,
Gave me back my life;
Not while I was awake,
But while I was asleep

Your deft fingers,
Your wisdom so deep,
Constant compassion ... relentless curiosity.
And your perfection lingers.

It is my turn now – Doctor Dan
To personally and family wide,
Thank you ... and Doctor Nate
For my return to the living,
And a loving life with my mate.

Coming Around

What?
Turn the other cheek,
Be meek,
To the dictates of a perverted society;
To he,
That makes a cuckold of me?

I think not!
No price is too cheap
For that value system.
They go with the sty
And smell of the swill,
That twice seen,
Makes up their characterless soul.

Ha! The rich can be warped
By assumed omniscience.
Their arrogance leads to
Unwitting caprophagy,
Toasted as elegance;
In stupid ignorance.

Let rogues rot in hell;
Not for their extracurricular deed,
But for spousal insensitivity,
Engendered by depravity,
Consummated in immorality.

Evening

There's a crescent moon barely holding water.
The blue is darkening into dusk.
I see the day's glimmer on the waters below,
And feel the shadows as they grow.

Jagged peaks, a chiaroscuro with the twilight,
The day is all but done;
Except for where it arises on another horizon,
Awaiting rebirth of the sun.

Here, I say goodbye to the day I have seen,
Goodbye to the sights of all living beings;
Goodbye to the creatures of the light
And Hello! – to the creatures of the night.

Why a melancholy air?
Why is there the burden of trepidation?
Perhaps the fear for a hidden mistake
That in the morning I should not wake.

But creation turns as it always has
And what goes around comes around again.
Tenuously, the living evolve
And round and round the world revolves.

Dream

To sleep is to dream,
Out of control –
tortuous, soothing, inspiring.
Mind's chaotic nature!
The present - the past,
A deranged jumble
Of real and imagination.
Departure from reality!

Oh! The gift of awakening!

Getting Old

I am getting older,
There's no question about that.
I just don't have the energy,
When my turn comes to bat.

Hell, I can't even leave home,
Let alone get to first.
I used to think about other things,
Now it's just beer to quench my thirst.

When the ump hollers strike,
I don't even see what goes by.
I can't hear a damn thing,
And I'm blind in one eye.

My hair is gone,
I can't reach my toes.
I've got bumps on my body,
And what I'm thinking about - who knows?

My sense of direction
Is right on the mark.
But you'd better show me the way home,
Before I depart.

Oh! My mind was quick,
Sharp as a tack.
I could talk myself out of trouble,
And never look back.

Well at least I have memories,
And can remember a thing or two.
Much more than those,
Is about all I can do.

I was strong as an ox,
When I was young and in my prime.
Now I am gasping for air,
No more feats of endurance to occupy my time.

Some ladies in my life showed up,
And away some went.
But you can rest assured,
It's on them, my money was spent.

Well I'm here today
And damned glad of it.
Being the head of the litter,
Beats sucking hind tit.

Diestic Contemplation

Grace softens the inner beast,
The storm that rages within.
The maelstrom of troublesome thoughts,
To live, evokes no requiem.

But where the Grace, where the Power
To strengthen the resolve?
The search for a viable continuum,
From the darkness to evolve.

A minute, an hour, a day of mental quietude,
A week, a month, a year of exactitude.
Is precision truly within reach,
Or just a fleeting attitude?

Is it in contribution
That we receive ablution;
Our life to give to another,
To feign a plausible solution?

Did the Omniscient exist prior to man,
Or is He a reduction of Pantheism?
A mere hook to hang your doubts on,
Or a simple anachronism.

Maybe awe required explanation,
A reason for the inexplicable.
A panacea for fear,
For demons inextricable.

Perchance this need
Did evoke creativity to spawn
A Supernatural to lay blame,
For the lack of a pristine dawn.

Or an inability to grasp
Nature's natural way,
An acceptance of ideality,
Without something else to say.

Did man create deistic ideation?
Is He a deification for man's ineptitude;
A cogently inspired crutch;
An egotistically desired beatitude?

Preposterous perceptions?
Pernicious putrefaction?
Execrable mentality,
For demented satisfaction?

The magnitude of such presumption!
Mental mendacity,
To even suppose
Man has that capacity!

Reflex ions

What's that cloud cover?
Is the sun waning before my eyes,
Or is my life fading?
I must try and realize,
Attempt to prioritize
My every endeavor.
Be smart, be clever!

My recollections ephemeral,
Words I cannot find;
They lurk in the shadows of my mind.
My thoughts extemporal.

Lucidity I ponder.
Will it be for me to grasp,
Or be out yonder?

My mentality to deteriorate.
An idea to infuriate.
What right to take my brain;
What compassion to see me strain
In my ebbing years reflecting,
Seldom objecting,
To iniquitous deeds.

The years went by
In an endless stream.
Not to question why
But to keep pace it would seem.
Now the months and weeks
Disappear like water down the drain;
Nothing lasts, nothing stays the same.

And of late, no change,
Nothing new to arrange.
The hours idle while I sit and wait
For that day, my inevitable fate.
Life I have been given,
And for that, I've striven,
Now life with death must I mate.

Hello Doctor!

Where for art though, great healers of the masses?
Probably on your yachts, sipping champagne from crystal glasses,
While all about you, health is draining
From those less fortunate who are often left paining.

Your arrogant demeanor and supercilious attitude,
Propel you to flatulent heights while you prescribe another platitude.
Your course is wrong as the future will prove.
It's the ache and turmoil you should try to sooth

Your time for frivolity may soon go,
As many regard you as their primary foe.
And unlike the phoenix, you shall not rise again,
As your time will come ... hubris has no friend.

Darkest Time of Day

The darkest time of the day,
Between zero and sleep.
Those moments when the unthinkable creep,
The ultimate solution.

But calming to your mind,
As an answer to all the stresses.
A void where bliss can exist,
No encroachment.

No darkened corners harboring guilt,
No woulda-coulda-shouldas,
No need for atonement,
For something you didn't do.

Your darkening sphere
Has no chinks to let light seep.
Your mind numbs out,
Perceived hallucinations rumble.

And finally, you cave to the other side.
In sleep only,
But not as you had imagined.
Another day plowed through – and then tomorrow.

Premonitions

Premonitions of doom cloud my mind.
Memories are confused.
Order is abused.
Ideation, unattainable.
Mental decline, pathology insidious?
Unquantifiable tangibly.

Is this old age?
Is this senility in its infancy?
Modicums of stress, chaotic.
Physical agility waning –
That's acceptable.
But my mind - must remain respectable!

On Notice

The parameters have been set,
My horizon is in sight.
No reason to worry,
No reason for fright.

My chores are at hand,
Explore all the possibilities
In research institutes,
All across the land.

No more vacillations,
Move ahead with direction
And avoid procrastinations.
Be discerning in my selections.

The click of the clock,
The inexorable passage of time
Mandates I take stock.
Drink from the chalice of wine.

Oh Wildwood
A ranch once owned in Colorado

Oh Wildwood, Wildwood, you are to me
What no place else could ever be.
Your moods, your song,
It is where I belong.

If I left you, my heart stayed there.
My soul will always float somewhere
Amongst your purple hills,
Your green, your snow and musical rills.

Though I long for you throughout the day,
It is a price that I have had to pay
To keep the peace with the one I love.
Perhaps I'll return some day –
On the wings of a dove.

Not Stopping?

Ever worried about not stopping,
When you can't even get started?
Ever worried about pooping,
When you haven't even farted?

It's all in your mind,
This thing called stress.
It builds logarithmically,
Causing undue duress.

Believe it or not,
There's more than one way out.
Put your head under a pillow,
Scream and shout.

An alternate panacea,
Might be liquor or wine.
A judicious use,
Will help over time.

All Around Us

The foggy bottom clears,
the cool air dries,
the red-winged blackbird
awakens its neighbors.
The reeds stir with morning breezes.
A deer treads softly
so as not to break the grass.
A larger critter may lowe
and in the distance,
a farmyard correspondence starts.

Is it just another day or a new beginning?
Both, you might say as the cycle turns.
What was yesterday may no longer be in the morn
and what is to be tomorrow may not be here today.

Life, a continuum in accordance with nature's laws;
butterfly wings or puppy's paws,
a Zephyr upon your cheek,
just a gentle reminder of the spectrum,
from the stronger to the meek.

What is to be gained through observation -
sensitivities to life and the beauty all around
and hopefully a love and appreciation
for our fleeting moments while here.

Be aware, have an open mind.
See with your soul!
Hear with your feelings!
Taste without fear!
Don't be blind,
Life is dear!

You Just Don't Know

You just don't know,
Unless you've been there.
The paucity of attraction,
The diminishing return on life's investments,
The scarcity of sensual sequences,
The absence of excitement.
You just don't know!

You just don't know
The roller-coastering
Catapulting you to the next apogee;
The tumultuous deflation to its antithesis.
Here today, gone tomorrow,
Its surcease incessant.
You just don't know!

You just don't know
If you really care.
Today or tomorrow,
Somnolence a palliative?
The mummification of elation,
From here to the last synapse.
You just don't know!

Adjust

What perils creep through the mind's open doors?
Doubts - goodness wanes,
Unsound reasoning leaning to the macabre,
Reasoning without foundation,
Logic and sanity gone.

Cerebral filters out of place
Disappearance of logic.
Games that no one wins.
Night is day, day is night
To sleep is to escape.

Not a verisimilitude, this aura,
Not without possibility, but likeliness not.
Ideation may portend the ridiculous,
Actuality need not follow.
Bend the mind toward light and right.

Grasp, learn, stir, mix and adjust,
It is to practicality that we must
Strive to weed the seed of anguish.
Accept that which we cannot turn to our favor.
Leave the rest to rust.

A Woman

A zephyr's caress, the shadow of a butterfly wing,
Rainbows undress her soul, to a vulnerability ...
A tenderness, there to find the character beneath,
Resiliency, love, stalwart ... gifts to bequeath.

What is Life?

Life is a waiting game
From the womb to the tomb,
Each day, never the same.

Or, life is an event
From when the fun had really begun,
And for you to wonder just where it all went.

Or maybe life is an orchestrated ordeal,
All exacted to see if you reacted
To a mysterious Almighty appeal.

Or maybe it is something just to titillate your yen.
At any rate, there is enough to sate,
Even the most curious of all men.

What we are Dealt

What there is to love,
Should be loved beyond compare –
Lest there is no love – anywhere.

What is seen,
Should be absorbed –
Lest sight be lost – Damocles sword.

What we hear,
Should not be a distraction –
Lest imperviousness – eliminates reaction.

What we touch,
Must touch our sensitivities –
Lest we succumb to proclivities.

What we say,
Must engender peace –
From discord, a surcease.

What we do,
Should be helpful to others –
Gratitude to ensue.

What we are dealt,
We must deal with –
Lest we never be dealt again.

Torn

What distant ephemeral memory
Stirs the heart within?
What chimerical fragrance
Deigns your design to sway
From cast templates
Of social mores?

Is it not the mind that dines
On things so fine,
As to sway the stoutest of intentions?
Is it not a figment of a long-lost dream
To roil the calm waters
To inappropriate dimensions?

Perhaps a whim not achieved,
Or a resolution not to be had.
Is there goodness in things deemed to be bad,
Or tortuous trails to be traveled
To perfidious ignominy?
Is love to last to infinity?

An answer is like a zephyr whispered,
Sensed, not felt, yet obviated
By the fact of life itself.
But that answer not accepted -
Is a wavering weak beacon;
A beckoning for a soul to weaken.

Time and Space

Is the object of our occupancy -
Of our little space here on earth,
Solely to languish in what it offers us,
Or to leave something of value and worth?

Are our exploits to be just for selfish reasons,
To be for our own self-aggrandizement?
Or perhaps more appropriately directed,
Towards society's timely refinement.

A natural stratification is mandatory;
A holistic hierarchal structured community
Where individuals and entities can coexist,
But not to the deprivation of individual opportunity.

Such should be our collective effort,
A miniscule step in the right direction;
A mark of acceptable legacy
To create a superior genetic selection.

A Mind Not at Peace

I cannot live with the sins that haunt me -
I cannot live and expect the sun to rise.
No heavenly light should shine upon me,
A Stygian darkness should occlude my way.
My knowledge miniscule,
Yet the burden overwhelming.
A cousin's husband to her sister's bed,
A brother to his brother's wife.
Not by he, but a cuckhold made of me,
And I anguished as a wittol!
Yet, guilty as the other, dare I cast aspersions?
The thought ergo the deed -
To not heed - the stultification of imagination.
What exceeds that form of hypocrisy
Which overtakes my mind to feign normality?
A God's way to torment those absent in following
A Path devoid of mental torture.
Caught in a maelstrom of a sodomitic society.
Animalistic in nature but devoid of survival acumen -
A contagion of moralistic depravity.
Anguish until death do us part.

Vis Vie
French: Live Life

Two pathways through life,
a straight one and the labyrinthine.
The former, less problematic perhaps,
but the latter - greater fulfillment.
Shed myopia – embrace its antithesis!
Tis better to run and envision,
than stagnate and deteriorate.

Reflections II

Taciturn to introversion, affliction, addiction or social
perversion,
Perhaps introspection ... mental rejuvenation.
Perspective, elective, objective, directive, collective.
The penultimate, fact or fiction.

Lesser and greater times,
Morning fragrance, soft blush, hush, beauty!
No words to describe,
Lost adjectives.

Corporeal magnetism
Intensifying, belying what greater exigencies.
Propinquity???
Muse - amuse ya - Perugia - use ya - excuse ya ...
So easily connected, but not with intention.
What order?
Not necessarily destiny.

Quixotic flail at a fading fantasy,
Or the budding birth of symphonic bliss.
Quagmire or maelstrom of emotional reflections.
The night tosses in perpetual perturbations.
Where the out,
Where the release,
Where the power,
For conceptual cease?

Frustrations, libations, flirtations, gyrations, machinations.
The solution is there ... but where?
The answer is union, spiritual, physical and solid.
But what path, what order, to uproot the stolid?

What stochastic process
To unleash the past?
Love's mysterious way,
Can anything last?

Dilemma?

Anatomically, I'm OK;
Chronologically, there's a disparity.
My two heads are not the same age.
Apparently, that's not a rarity.

I've thought about it a good deal
And after careful consideration,
I think I'm pretty normal.
There is no aberration.

For it seems that as I have grown,
I've shunned good advice
And plunged madly forward,
Thinking with my device.

There have been some troubles along the way,
And down the paths I've been led.
But I've always tried to be careful,
Wherein I've put my head.

Twilight

Beyond your horizon lies your twilight,
A bare awareness in younger years,
But insidiously approaching.
One that only you must face,
Drawing nigh at an unknown pace.

Your reflections of highs and lows
Crowd the years,
As they seem like yesterday.
And they were, and will continue;
An unending tomorrow.
Live! Think not of time to borrow.

But your days are finite
And the bell rings on occasion.
A TIA, a missed plan for a certain day,
A test of endurance – failed.
Logicality may wane
And there may be greater emotional pain.

A natural preparedness that we try to ignore.
A clarity of vision that we wish wasn't there.
Is there an obscure message being delivered,
Whose meaning will clear with dusk?
Do we hide from life's shadows, in the dark?
Or do we just go out and play in the park?

A mental, moral dilemma,
For there are demands that we plan
For an event not sought.
The weights of responsibilities;
Sort the greed from the need,
… to appease your seed.

Temptation

Life, like a Lacy Florentine,
So deliciously tasty,
But Oh! So brittle!

Crumbling on a whim,
Irrevocable chards!
Bits of succulence –
But not holistic!

Hell No!!!

I'm not alright – never have been.
My life has been a fright,
One missed point after another.
Few things done right.

Cute memories to shed a tear by?
Get serious!
Tears, a lachrymal expulsion,
Placating emotions of the imperious.

You want to know what and why I write,
To vent my spleen and be truthful re my plight?
Born a depressive and exhibited through life,
Woefully passed on – my contribution – a blight!

Suicidal at ten and then at fifty-five again.
Came close, but intervention prevailed.
And how many times in between?
Maybe old age will terminate the trail.

Old Things

Things that you want to share, never stay the same.
They lose their importance over time.
The evoked emotions wane
And sift back to your reverie.

You come across that hidden page,
Put aside for an important occasion;
The picture or article, so very sage,
Its history now, few care.

Except for you and your memories stimulated,
The feeling is still there.
Your head nods with moments contemplated,
And you re-file it for another day.

The Littered Trail

Why we can't see
What we have wrought
Is surely chicanery
On purposeful thought?
Angels weep
Ore desecrated lands.
Miscreant deeds
By deceitful hands.

Too late
For restitution,
Our sins continue
Without ablution.
Where the virginal beauty?
Where of unadulterated peace?
No longer attainable,
Accept without surcease!

Anything that smacks
Of intellectuality
Lies fallow,
As unattainable reality.

Hello Again

You sound so cool,
So detached.
An affair here, there,
Soon dispatched.

That's not the girl I knew.
A facade that slowly grew?
Belied perhaps by that tremulous voice,
Questioning ...
The girl I knew will always be there.

Gentle, caring, giving, full of love,
But protective of self.
With that admonition, Beware!

A ruthless aloofness?
I think not!
A salve on heart scars?
Perhaps that's what she's got.

And so it should be for all to see
That your heart is not to squander.
You are your own thoughts,
And hidden ... others are left to ponder.

Keep them tight and secure.
Don't let others invade
what's yours and yours alone,
until decisions are finally made.

Let yourself out for others to glimpse.
Whet their appetites, but keep a tight rein
lest in emotional confusion,
your compulsivity, you'll disdain.

You have a love of immense proportions.
Protect it, keep it, but keep it in motion.
Stagnation is disuse and leads to regressions.
Be ready for the one with proper devotion.

Dejection

The fire is no longer burning!
The dreams are ashes now,
No more yearning.

The years have slipped by;
By design,
Or by mistake.

Too late to ask why!

I've had gains,
I've had losses.
From abyss to being remiss,
Can't examine the causes.

My life's jewels are gone,
One to heaven, the other also.
No time for another dawn.

Oh well! Such was life.
Work a little,
Play a little.
Mask the strife.

Inner self

Inner self,
Screaming to get out;
Afraid to venture.

Clouds shroud doorway,
Occluded through time;
Waisted, running out!

Longing to burst forth;
Petals on blossoms,
Glee to free.

Fall approaching,
Opportunities wane;
Doors shut inexorably!

Think for yourself

There never was a word spoken or a song sung,
That pleased all the people.
There never was a church built,
That had the perfect steeple.

Would it all be so simple,
But acceptance is in man's mind.
Anything less,
We'd all be one of a kind.

It was not His way to make us as such.
How dull and how boring!
Stagnation would reign supreme,
For our minds and hearts, no soaring.

Is that the world that should be -
All to be one way?
No differences to complain,
No one else to have their say?

How banal our existence.
Let expressions proliferate;
If found not acceptable,
With the less content, commiserate.

What an uninteresting lot
We would all be,
If unanimous decisions,
Were all we could see.

Think for yourself.
To your thoughts be true.
Don't be led, but instead,
Originality should be a part of you.

Feel Every Dream

I just saw a shooting star,
Not too near, and not too far,
In a night full of air like cotton;
You know, like those nights not forgotten.

Like you used to remember
In summer, not winter and December.
The lazy breezes like velvet on your skin.
You do remember, how it used to have been?

But it still is, just think
How it used to be and drink
The memories so full of flavor.
Let your mind wander, every drop, savor.

And realize before it's too late,
What you think is gone and was great,
Still enfolds you; as you dream it must.
Life is here - and hasn't turned to dust.

June 2008

Trepidation over proposed move back to Rancho Santa Fe, CA where unhappiness had prevailed.

Will Rancho divide and conquer one more time?
Will I be left without a life sublime?
Do excesses warp the mind,
Blinding sensitivities so hard to find?
Does light turn to dark as terminal night?
Will a once rich harvest turn to a blight?

Will the sun dim each morn
Or the song bird sing with scorn?
Will rain drops be cloudy
And quiet moments become rowdy?
Will all that we have worked for,
Wane, drift away to be no more?

I start the trip back with huge trepidation,
Doubts cloud my mind evoking hesitation.
Why do I jump just to appease
When standing firm is the position I should seize?
Why can't I look at it as a bright new beginning,
Instead of the harbinger of beauty thinning?

Do I fear from past fear itself, lurking to jump at me?
What quirk in my mind suggests that yore will now be?
Are there subtle suggestions that I am sensing
Or a feeling of a relationship, tensing?
The mere thought of that inscrutable pain,
Is far more than my psyche can tame.

No question, my life would be through.
I guess from that deck of cards, the Joker I finally drew.
My children, all grown now, and theirs growing too,
Some will benefit - they think – if they only knew.
I always loved them – a good father / husband, I did try.
It's too sad to even ponder – so I say Good Bye!

It Ain't So Bad Being Man

A world that turns in perfect circles
Is nothing short of a miracle.
Why then suppose so blithely,
That you should never be hysterical?

If upside down you should find yourself
With no more aspirations,
Then look depression right in the eye,
And consider a reincarnation.

Rather than human,
What should you choose to be,
A sluggish cephalopod,
Or a sought-after hard wood tree?

A plant that's doomed to agent orange,
A worm in the terra-firmament,
Eaten by a ravenous robin;
Then to pass as excrement?

The choices, there're a myriad
And go on ad infinitum,
And only you can make up your mind;
The meaning of life - desideratum.

But there is one fact without a doubt!
Only humans can enjoy the pleasures
Of sunsets, moons, loons and lagoons,
And all of life's other treasures.

On Aging

My eyes are diming with age,
A thought that's difficult to bear.
Where has the sky of the West gone,
What of that irretrievable blue?

With my vision, so my hearing.
Melodic orchestrations of avian friends
Now silenced form coveted senses,
An almost unbearable travesty.

Freedom of ambulation?
Hills, dales, varied trails,
Such a part of my soul;
Now relegation to sidewalks.

Acceptance, an impossibility
To sanction life's dwindling facets.
What then, fight on in futility,
Till dreams become reality once more.

The Years Pass On

Images of yesterday, ebbing, gone,
Like shadows, moving on.
Deep memories, clear now;
Early skies brighten.

Loves past, rekindled,
Flames fanned and mingled.
Sorrows saddened by guilt or reason,
What trepidations we've traveled with!

Moments of clouded courage
Leading to wanton demurrage.
High cost of hesitation;
Squandered plethoric opportunities.

Search vainly for light!
Illuminate encroaching night.
A modicum of respect gleaned
From deeds visualized by others.

Depression - part of reality,
The journey to finality.
Surely pride must prevail in others,
Even if not perceived by self.

Plight

White is black!
No, black is white!
What is wrong with you?
You're not alright!

A multiplicity of contradiction!
Dark begets light,
Or so it would seem;
If you make it through the night.

You awake!
And if – what then?
Guess what you get to do -
Start all over again.

Remember

Let your mind drift, just for a moment,
To those lost, a brother, husband or wife.
Remember those special times,
Unrepeatable, only but for the memories,
Indelible to last your whole life.

Was it yesterday or last year,
Or maybe years past?
Did it involve others,
Or was is just the two of you,
In an abbreviated setting that couldn't last?

Whatever the situation, be Oh, so thankful,
That you are here to savor this day.
Look upon it as a gift,
That it can become part of the present,
And not something that has to fade away.

Your Heart

Flicker, flicker!
Watch the flame grow higher,
But watch your step,
Lest you fall into the fire!

Dolts

Vainglorious dolts who exalt over a self-perceived lofty societal level,
Ought to examine the rungs of the ladder they've trod upon,
To see if they are still there for their eventual descent,
Lest in times of strife they find their perch abruptly gone.

Up, down, round and round, it matters little your evasive action.
You cannot escape your shadow no matter how hard you try.
Cursory, platitudinous, banalities used for social elevation,
Are but transparent, perfidious acts that they will be remembered by.

Where to From Here

Mental alacrity -
Still within sight.
But no one listens,
On age there's a blight.

Perish the thought
That some utterance should be sage.
A futile attempt
To socially engage.

And what a ridiculous effort,
As a respected poet, to endeavor
To once again,
Be philosophically cleaver.

"Oh God, he's at it once more!"
There just may be some wisdom
In - or between the lines,
That isn't some banal aphorism.

Too soon as time slips by,
The more relevant will be swept under
For survivors to ponder;
Pearls of sanity, evoking wonder

Frustrated Horticulturist

Why do plants, that have a natural proclivity to live,
Upon acquisition and though I try,
Manage to change priorities,
And give up and die?

I water as I should,
And fertilize accordingly to Hoyle.
I prune judiciously,
And take great care with the soil.

I'm a naturalist by heart,
But try as I might,
Giving tender love and care,
There is never new growth in sight.

My fruit split early!
Dehiscence is rife!
My leaves show deficiencies!
No end to my strife!

I truly think that I shall
Give them just one more chance.
And if life they'll not live for me,
They'll nare get another glance.

To a condo I'll move,
All landscaped with rock,
And horticulture be damned.
All my tools I'll hock.

To the store I will go
And a garden I'll not try -
I'll buy produce and flowers
Until the day I die.

Why, One Day

What do I look for,
An easy evacuation,
A release,
And nothing more?

A departure from reality,
An escape from the haunts,
To a nothingness future?
Leave emotionality?

Why continue a farcical life?
Nothing to be gained, nothing lost.
Those coming after,
Will gain from my strife.

So, adios now!
Maybe today, maybe tomorrow.
Who really gives a rat's ass?
Societal laws do not allow.

Disgust

Metaphorically speaking, you're an ass.
In actuality, you have no class.
And before I am through
I want to make it quite clear to you
That everything you do is crass.

You really are a boor,
Of that I am certainly sure.
You are undeniably crude;
Your demeanor is lewd
And for your genetic structure, there's no cure.

You are parasitic,
Cerebrally arthritic,
Devoid of sensitivity.
Your destiny a declivity,
To be eventually autolytic.

Is there any saving grace
To the tiny little place,
You occupy on this earth?
You are met with mirth
As a member of the human race.

So, in eloquent summation,
For you there's no laudation,
Just a totally robust
Amount of disgust
For a pathetic aberration.

What's Better?

Is it not better to know a little about a lot,
Than a lot about a little,
To be able to dodge hazardous ways,
And avoid life's spittle?

Is it not better to be able to speak your tongue
With an educated degree of precision,
Than to needlessly fret about
A critic's unwanted excision?

Is it not better to look the part,
And harmoniously blend,
Than to be garish,
And your ways on the morrow to mend?

And one other thought comes to mind.
It's far better to have civility;
Give the others their due,
And be known for social desirability.

A boor is a clod at best,
Totally lacking in refinement.
A braggadocio and buffoon,
Seeks only self-aggrandizement.

Trail to Nowhere

Meandering aimlessly, day by day, night be night.
Each week an extension of last – forgotten.
A month, Spring, Summer, Fall – who is aware?
Certainly not I, as incidents seem non-existent.

A light of excitement, not in my existence,
As long as there are no dimensions to happiness.
Measurement of time by ticking of the clock,
Not episodic moments of memorable bliss.

Ha! That it should be possible to lock away in mind.
Years will move, time will pass, calendars will click,
Away their pages until finality prevails –
And the path started, winds up as a no-where trail.

Divisional Man

Road to hope, malleability or rigidity?
Contrive to divide, categorize, improvise.
Minds wander, squander,
Wearing, tearing, creating, mating.
To divide, each dividend smaller.

Mind, finite magnitude or growth to cope?
Cerebral precocity, erasure,
Directional, seizure.
Finiteness yet dynamically dimensional;
Implicational of intentional.
Algorithm to lunacy.

Which came first, mind or thought that we can change?
Not possible! Thought emanates from the mind.
Phantasm of mental mendacity, mind control,
Yet we assume that we can control the mind.
What controls, some inner piece of the mind?

But that is the mind.
Is the mind self-correcting?
Carnage, reduction from our mistakes?
Cognitive power to effect change?
Can one part of the mind change that very same part,
A challenge, a mental maelstrom the mind shouldn't start.

The Far Side of Sanity

It seems so far, far away.
What a long trek back,
If it can be made.
I knew it long ago,
Seems almost forgotten.
I wonder if it's for me to know.

A calmness, no turmoil.
Placidity – seems unreal.
Maybe it is.
Maybe it was the norm,
Like how you felt
Before you were born.

Nonsensical feelings,
Sense out of chaos,
When there shouldn't be.
Aberrational urges!
Societal contradictions!
Emotional surges!

This is not to be harbored.
It's just not normal.
Cerebration screams for truth.
Evasive – out of touch,
Almost tangible.
It's just too much.

I wonder!
Encroaching age, mind addling,
But to know no peace?
A fearful price!
Life has been good,
Now, however,
Not nice!

Life's a Limerick

When I was born in thirty-five,
That's the year I started to thrive.
My life before me was already set,
Not for me to question or rue the debt.
Just prevail and try to stay alive.

Down hallways of trials and tribulations,
And others of rewards and laudations.
The morrow brings the unknown;
Whether in obscurity or at home,
Handling praise or accusations.

And unto a teen a man is born
To confront the world and limit scorn.
Loneliness, perceived or real,
Needing a reason to feel.
Coping - from a family he is torn.

Decisions are upon him,
None to be taken lightly or on a whim.
Performance is now the order of the day,
If in front of his peers he tries to stay,
And find a mate which he has to win.

Examples to be set,
Live a life without regret.
Lead, even if feeling inadequate to do so,
But it is through life, which he must go.
It is the good times that he must collect.

And teach his progeny, right from wrong,
By deed, example, and even song.
The burdens weigh heavy,
The hazards – a tax levy.
But the rewards, a garden of glee and green lawn.

And watch the children grow,
And watch the children go,
To carry on another generation in another land.
Accomplishments and fatigue are now at hand,
And now life has become subtly slow.

Eighty years I've been on this planet
And for my few sorrows, I would like to re-plan it.
It has been a lovely ride,
Not one I could chide.
If possible, I'd scan it, not feasible – damn it!

Self-snuff

Why today,
Why not tomorrow?
Why tomorrow,
Why not today?
What little difference it makes.
Each day a prolongation
Of today.
Attitude adjustments --- –
There are none!

Introversion

The hazy days of summer float like reflections on still water.

Why can't our minds react accordingly?
Long lengths of languid lulls,
Interspersing turbulent, troubled times,
Guaranteeing serene rhythmicity to roiling waters.

A cacophonous concoction of mingled emotions;
Dulling, desultory passions drifting aimlessly without direction;
Past, present, imperfect, pluperfect, life a pasquinade.
Erasing racing years, an effort in futility;
Accept, pursue not prescience, prioritize the present.

Ah! Were it possible to correct the errors!
We are a summation of all that passes,
Making us uniquely different from all the masses.
We are who we are for those we can enthrall,
A protoplasmic blip on the cosmic screen ---frailties and all.

About A Poet

To those who write a line of wit
And think their mind is aptly quick,
May their brains be appropriately lit;
Even if it's just with a candlestick.

They vie for time
With a simple rhyme;
But fail for a line,
Which is borderline.

They thumb their nose
At conventional prose,
And what do you suppose,
Delusion means that anything goes.

People nod with diluted praise,
And vigorous hopes for limited days.
They ponder how much one must pay,
To change the bore and his rhyming way.

Well, nothing will end it,
So, grin and bare a bit.
Although it ain't exactly fit,
There's probably no end to all his shit.

Verdens Ende
Norwegian: Worlds End

I see no reason to continue this façade.
 I see no reason to continue this chicanery,
Or continue this pasquinade.

What ominous cloud enveils us?
What darkness occludes our vision
To perceive what entails us?

What hints of disaster prevails over us?
What do I have left to bequeath?
What glimpses of promises
To enlighten the horizons of those yet to come?

None!

Le Bouton

The button of finality
Transports beyond the pain,
Beyond the realization that we lost our aim,
Allowing permanent escape
From banality.

Poussée le Bouton,
Pourquoi non?

The end to all failures,
Outnumbering gains.
Correct route not taken, wrong lanes
Leading to grief and guilt,
N'est pas, le meileur ?

Poussée le Bouton,
Pourquoi non?

Yes! A coward's way to take,
The end at last!
No more thoughts about the past!
Cessation of appeasement!
Just another big mistake!

Poussée le Bouton,
Pourquoi non?

No plans for the morrow,
No excuses to make,
No more life to fake -
All is clear now!
There will be little sorrow.

Poussée le Bouton,
Pourquoi non?

Look Thee Not

Explore not over thin ice,
Lest in seeking
There'll be reciprocity
In wounding.

The ice may crumble!
Your role of the dice,
Bereft of acumen;
A non-rectifiable stumble.

Dérèglement

Why the sky so blue,
Why the dark of the depth?
All scientific exactitudes!
Ponder less of yonder.
Perplex upon the esoterica
Of today's tumultuous vicissitudes.

Musings on Getting Old

So many things to do,
So many places to see;
So many of my loved ones to tell,
That they mean so much to me.

The Reaper winks a beckoning call.
Alas! A call I must try and resist.
Let me spend my time with my Mary,
And tell Him to cease and desist.

But my chest races at night,
My torso reacts with frightening pain.
I function not as well,
Strength ebbs, loss of aim.

I must hide how I feel
Until a more convenient time.
I tremble with dread,
Yet my life has been sublime.

Even my memory fades,
Yester lore escapes me now,
Except for the long-gone minutia.
The furrows increase on my brow.

If the slide is ahead,
And there is no turning back,
Let the world know,
That I have loved without slack.

I have been a gentle man,
A caring, compassionate, good mate.
There's some who doubt,
But that is their mistake.

To live with and be consumed by!
I cannot reach those who don't understand,
Nor should I have tried,
For they will sport their mental contraband.

Well, ramble on, I must not,
For time is fleeting and it's rest I need.
My life, should it end abruptly,
Was one filled with love, indeed!

Slow Down

Why should I take time,
For people who don't take time for me?
Why should I stress,
When stressin' is a waste of time you see?

If I wake up in the morning,
That's a good way to start my day.
Earn a dollar,
And ain't got no bills to pay.

Eat a little when I'm hungry,
Don't make a God of my gut.
Eat on some schedule?
Get yerself in a rut.

No, life's pretty easy
Ifn' you jest don't fret.
Take it as it comes – nice and slow.
And don't break a sweat.

Musings on Aging

Is it early morning fog
or just the haze of the years?

I remember when
the sky was brighter.
I remember when
the rain drops were wetter,
flower blossoms were more intense
and true love made more sense,
special foods had a greater flavor,
music was truly music to my ears.
but now all that is muted.

It is as we go through life
and I guess that is what is best suited.
The horizons are closer
the waning years seem to increase with speed,
my heart seems to get heavier
and the dawn and dusk seem to get closer.

Simple chores now seem like arduous tasks
and a meal preparation seems unnecessary.
It is easier to stand up in the kitchen
and eat a can of cold beans
then to have to labor over pots
and pans and accompanying spices.

Why is it that last year's roses
were more abundant and fragrant and prettier?
Am I losing my touch?

I look back at what I perceived were great accomplishments
and now realize that they were just mundane,
in the scheme of things.
Like a piece of ice, we once were,
crisp and hard and resilient.
The world could skate upon us
and barely scratched the surface.

Through the years we soften
and our character flows away from us – melting.
We are less stalwart, less gregarious,
less capable of interesting others.
Our appearance starts to look like a wart,
wrinkled and calloused and ineffectual.
The sun does come up and create shadows,
not as crisp and vibrant as in the past,
but they still march across the wall and indicate – really nothing at all.
Melancholia persists
and I suppose it will until the end of the path is reached .

Act as You Feel

If you think you are as old as you are,
Then your thoughts have gone astray by far.
Tis far better you not act as you aught,
By acting according to your thought.

For to behave as a sage said was wise,
Might easily lead to an early demise.
Better yet, live as you feel;
Let each dream have a fulfilling appeal!

223

A Bipolar's Supplication

Oh, that thou could ride the high,
Avoiding the bottomless abyss.
A mind exploding with wealth,
Not a cerebration to miss.

The sweetness of dreams,
The fragrance of youth.
Daylight evidenced,
The essence of truth!

Feats unimpeded
By failing strength.
Soaring endeavors,
To life's intended length.

Not to be buried
In that downward spiral.
An insidious descent,
To dejection – gone viral!

Descry Love

Can you recognize love?
I think not!
It goes way beyond
What you've forgot.

Perception possible?
Not likely!
Clouded by history,
Dreamt of nightly.

What then went down,
Episode so terrible?
Exsanguination,
So inexecrable?

Tales untold,
Parts of the past,
But whose effects,
Are there to last.

Think Good Times

Think about the good things, not the bad.
Think about the happy moments, not the sad.
Think about the moments of utter bliss,
That I know you and I had.
And think about the wonderful times that we will miss,
When we allow ourselves to reminisce?

Encroaching Horizons

If you can wake up each morning recognizing -
The need for spirituality,
The demand for vitality,
The maintenance of your physicality,
And the exercising of your intellectuality,
Your diminishing pathway will be less agonizing.

225

Women

A woman by any other name would be a misnomer.
It would be like saying the Babe or Bonds never hit a homer.
There are some things that are so obvious in life,
That to try and deny them will cause nothing but strife.

By virtue of carrying that much acclaimed name,
They've become so unique that in nature, nothing can be the same.
There is no need to banter and orate, but just remember,
You simple have to admit and succumb to a superior gender.

Firstly, the implications are simple,
To start with, somewhere, she simply has a dimple.
From there, their bodies are absolutely sublime,
Metamorphosed, sculptured, matured, over time.

A blemish or a wrinkle will tell a thousand tales.
To have less - would be like corduroy without wales.
It would be like un-blown desert sand,
Having not met nature's demand.

And of their mind, there is perpetual lateral thinking
That constantly gives a man that feeling of sinking.
There is no definition to "can't"
And an accurately uttered occasional "shant".

Their energies are absolutely beyond explanation,
Beyond a man's most comprehensive contemplation.
Whether it's socializing, children or an athletic endeavor,
Their rejuvenation capabilities go way beyond just being clever.

Their artistic machinations and Christmas tree trims,
Speak of an imaginative creativity and unexplored whims.
A living charade, you never know where they really are,
Try to guess and you'll be wrong by far.

And get them angry or just unreasonably irritated,
And like an alligator that's constipated,
Their teeth get bared and can slash and tear,
Eviscerate … cut you anywhere.

Leave you questioning your manhood,
Contemplating other things that are really not good.
Bewildered, confused, from the gallows you wish to be hung,
All because of their malicious, melliferous, miscreant tongue.

And then in a heartbeat, it would seem to be over,
But they never forget, even if bedded in clover.
A bit of advice … don't ever, ever rest,
'Cause their gender will get you and it won't be in jest.

You may cry or you may smile.
You are a toy for them to beguile.
They can ring your emotions,
Like typhoons to oceans.

So, try to be calm,
Say a prayer or psalm.
There is nothing you can do,
For with you, … they are never though.

Chicken Liver

When I was but twenty-five,
I had limited vision,
An undeveloped perception.
Now at the age of sixty-two
I have lived a little,
that is true.

But what is life without hills and dales,
Peaks and valleys,
And some outrageous trails?
A tragedy or two and love sublime,
All fills the mind
With depth and an attitude.

Warranted, perhaps not,
But who is in my mind,
Who looks through my eyes,
Who has the right
To dictate ... and under what guise?

Unique to myself,
That's what I am.
An unquantifiable entity,
Not to be parsed by man.

A gift to myself first!
To myself be true,
Lest I try to live the life of another;
And fail and have to start anew.

Theory of Creativity

The composer tells stories with his musicality.
The artist tells a story with his palette.
The poet tells stories with his words,
And the sculptor tells a story with his mallet.

The architect with his design,
The musician with a fife,
The inventor with imagination,
The whittler with a knife.

Creativity is within!
It just has to be awakened;
If not nudged now and then,
It will soon be forsaken.

Strength

Things of before,
Are no more,
Perhaps by Divine intervention.

So, dwell thee not
On yester lore,
Concentrate on less apprehension.

Perturbed

A long walk in my dark
May show me where I am supposed to be.
I seem to have forgotten,
Where is my destiny.

Is my soul detached and on its own?
Is my mind out of sync with what is real?
Is the world around me as it ought to be?
Questions, questions … just how should I feel?

Don't Leave a Hot Woman

Don't leave any hot woman alone,
Kiss your connection goodbye.
You're as deep in her heart
As the legs on a fly.

Your memory, a candle's dying smoke,
Wafting, to an inevitable dead end;
As her unquenchable fire,
To another's demise, will send.

Insatiable, unconquerable, do not attempt.
An effort spawned in hell
With no rewards to keep.
Scars to death's knell.

Double Standard

A rogue and a ram,
My boy will grow to be a man.
For moral pluralism there's no cure,
My girls are going to be chaste and pure!

Generational Changes

To the top of the peak
I did try to climb,
But was thwarted by life,
And apathy sublime.

And where did this malady arise?
Why from my heritage, I presume.
As I never accepted the right guidance,
As it was nil, I was to assume.

Nil, 'cause it didn't exist?
Or unrecognizable in form.
Why were parental attempts inept?
Because then, that was the norm!

What transition came to play,
That contact was finally made?
Evolution necessitated change,
Habits to expunge and finally to fade.

Maybe now, progeny will excel,
Having emotional assistance when needed,
And inner talents will prevail,
And past attempts exceeded.

Why, What?

Oh, that my existence should sink to such an ignominious level,
Or that the deprivations of aspirations
Should gray a sky of blue;
And otherwise obscure a cloudless creation!

What keeps the flicker illuminated?
Is the love for another of sufficient abundance,
To keep the light aglow,
Obviating exorbitance?

Or that the diminution of time immortal
Might assuage the trepidation of dislocation.
Is there to be a creation of a soothing balm
By the inevitability of continuation?

Or will the centrifugal force
Of celestial rotation
Fling aside negativity,
Engendering a harmonious explanation?

As I ponder the out yonder,
It gives me pause to realize that relative to space,
We move a thousand miles per hour - in a circle.
Dizzying through life at a terrible pace.

And we wonder why our hearts are a-whirl!
Ah! The fog of knowledge.

Good-Bye Creativity

What is it that dies within you,
As the years creep on?
An inability to vocalize emotions, –
To wallow unspoken of a nonpareil, devotion?

Why does creativity painfully wane,
When it previously bubbled spring-like?
Like an arid desert now, desiccated!
Torment, not to be conciliated.

Nostalgia, ne'er to be revisited,
Harbingers of what's to come?
Memories of yore.
Inevitable closure on life before.

A logarithmic conclusion
To the ellipse of life!
We depart antithetically as begun,
Precipitous fall from sight.

The Darker Side of Light

Manic man,
Satanic fan,
Overheated pan.
Societal ban,
Eliminate élan.
Improbable, "I can",
Inevitable also-ran.

Dark side of light,
Nightly fright.
Love's blight,
Inures the sight.
No force or might,
From abyss or height,
Makes it right.
Talk, out or within,

Do good or sin,
Infernal din,
Cacophonous kin,
Lead, not tin.
Efficacious gin,
Serendipitous win.

Light heart, rare.
Others stare.
Round appears square.
If only you dare,
Eyes glare,
Cerebral tear,
Not fair.

Run is done!
No fun in the sun!
Race not won!
Weighs like a ton!
Truth not pun!
Don't sting, stun!
Finality, gun!

Bipolarity

I'm not solar,
I'm bipolar.
And I get pissed when I please.
I get irritated
When I get constipated,
And when pollen makers me sneeze.

On the other hand, I'm as cheery as a daisy
And I drive people quite crazy,
Because I laugh a great deal.

I try and beguile
With my charming smile,
Because that's just the way I feel.

What path?

You ponder: You see the horizons pass day to night.
But what is in between, a continuing compromise
Of flowers for sage, weeds for age?
The truth eludes verities, mockery is water – flowing.

Has no one seen beyond, beyond; or is it unobservable?
Are years in bondage down the path of no return,
The inevitable lockstep into oblivion,
A way for those living to end their miniscule existence?

Is life really a decay of one's fundamentality,
A method of interior corrosion rusting to the surface,
To sacrifice the structural rigidity of skeletal frame?
Is all this really the epitaph on the grave of being?

Supreme Power

Beauty starts with Nature,
And Nature never ends.
Man's nimiety, a dark cloud!
There will be no amends!

Arrogance unfettered!
Expiation, a vain attempt!
Creation of betterment?
Pathways to contempt!

A mere blip on horizons,
Insignificant, our lives.
Nature – the Supreme Power!
Time thrives!

And There Goes The Sun

To the other
side where the day has just begun.
Earth, slowly on her axis spins ...
There, daylight again begins.
12 hours, balance from light to dark;
Without which, life would be so stark.
Man's contribution, minuscule.
Natural events control the rule.

That we should presume otherwise,
Will be our downfall and our demise.

All Rise

"All rise," Let humility somehow prevail;
Lest we fail, and end our trail.
intoned the bailiff; a roar ensued from moving bodies.
And there he strode in his great flowing robe.
Bespeckled and austere, imposing and severe,
Waiting to rule as his conscience would dictate;
The attorney's trepidations on how he might cogitate.

The jury quietly and nervously await
For evidence to accumulate at a staggering rate.
Will the supply of witnesses never abate?
Facts, times, dates, enough to totally sate
The over-burdened mind and memory's closed gate.

The day drones on pierced by piques of interest.
Rarely a chuckle to wrinkle the smooth oration.
Mellifluous scrapple, plausibly digested.
Prosecution, defense, completely unflappable,
Both striving for testimony trappable.

Fierce, cajoling, manipulative in their relentless attack,
Neither giving and inch nor willing to step back.
Both maneuvering from tack to tack,
Exercising their idiosyncratic knack
To pillar or remove from the potential rack.

Deemed by the jury guilty or not,
The system might be flawed,
But it's the best in the world,
Empowerment by the government
To negate their allegations with verbiage twirled.

237

Our civic duty is done
And to home we must run;
To live, work and play in freedom wrung
By bells of toil and standards hung
In a democracy that's the greatest … under the sun.

Laryngitis Rx
After pertussis in my seventies

You tell me not to talk,
Like a canary not to sing,
An owl not to hoot,
A bell not to ring.

You tell me not to talk.
How can I communicate
With those that I love,
And those I might hate?

You tell me not to talk …
An impossible thing!
Rushing water doesn't gurgle?
A ball of twine has no string?

As a doctor you should know
You can't stifle what's innate;
It's abnormal at best,
A request that doesn't rate.

As a doctor you should know
That elephants trumpet,
Coyotes howl,
And a harlot is a strumpet.

As a doctor you should know …
Your edict is completely preposterous!

Numbers   11/12/13

Numeric-logicality,
I suppose this day should be significant;
Because it is eleven, twelve, thirteen.
Does the cosmos really care?
It preceded the concept of numbers!

Insignificant blips of protoplasmic energy,
Failing, failing, failing to really do anything.
Individually racing towards oblivion,
To be measured as dust.

Molecules grasping to hang on to adhesion,
Keeping the bubble intact.
Why? Pointless endeavors,
As we wind up as some artifact.

Stuff:

Take me back to when my children were happy,
Take me back to when all was serene.
Don't let anything else come up,
Don't let anything intervene.

Oh my goodness!
Take me back to when correctness was not always an issue,
To when actions were based on spontaneity,
To when an arrow leaving the bow,
Found its way without some conceptual blemish.

To when our aim was not some premeditative move,
But engendered out of emotional reflex,
Out of an innate desire to do what's right,
And not out of some compendium's index

Why is the Why?

Why is the "Why" part of our daily vernacular?
Is it to try and explain the mundane or the spectacular?
Do we really need to ponder into the abstract,
In order to arrive at memories, we'd like to retract?

Perhaps to justify and explain the exigencies of life,
A futile attempt to avoid inner strife.
Or maybe yet, to try in vain
To rationalize that which causes us pain!

Should we not embrace the reality of the now,
Rather than retrospectively rationalizing of just how.
A good look on the morrow of what has happened today,
Just may be the salvation of a conscience gone astray.

If our life is to be judged on the summation of misdeeds,
Then where is the room for extolling the succeeds?
It is not the accumulation of nays that we should embrace,
But lighten our load by our accomplishments to trace.

And by there doing we can perfect our movements
Toward that which prospectively encourages improvements.
Let the "Why's" lead us forward toward an enlightened betterment,
And not to burdensome baggage precipitating our detriment.

Ego and The Creative Spirit

It has been said,
"Only ego drives the pen."
If so, are there no lessons to be learned
By Kipling, Keats and Burns?

Is all poetry blather,
Merely egotistic yammer;
Words for empty minds,
As a noisy anvil by a hammer?

Is it also ego
That drives the artist's brush;
The musician, to create joyous song,
As heard from the Thrush?

Or perhaps Mozart, Hayden and Bach,
Were emptying their egos on the score
For nothing but a catharsis,
And meant for nary more.

If so, that to be true,
Then it was an id driven ego's motivation,
That enabled our creative spirit
To spawn our cultural creation.

A Stranger in My Mind

Who knows me?
Certainly not myself!
I live alone!
I cry detached.

Why? I know not.
'Cause of someone I forgot?
Paper thin emotions.
No strength therein.

I wander – always have.
No anchor or guiding light.
Senseless directions
Lead to a vacuum …

Sucking for hope,
An elusive entity.
I have everything,
But peaceful serenity.

Just Please

A sophisticate, I am not;
Unequivocally, I assure you.
My heart is where the sky has no end -
The milky way joining the two blues.

Yesterday and today, a blend in time.
The prairie grass, bedding a new-born foal,
Meadow larks and all others,
Lullabies, soothing the soul.

Oh, that my days should cease
Without a long last look
At the wonders of the west,
And a gurgling brook.

The waters that hold so much!
Reflections of clouds and sun,
Tintinnabulations for the mind.
Images of trout on the run.

The lofty mountains,
Their majesty and lure.
The meadow-spotted valleys,
An encompassment, so secure.

The Creative Mind

The Palace of Poetry and Prose,
Palette for the poetical words.
License for pixilation,
Colors of day and night, dull and bright,
Like candy store, hardware store;
Nails, washers, tools, gadgets, widgets.
English, rich in meaning, immense in feeling.
Lexicon to form tapestry,
Ideation to sculpt verbal picture,
Wordy invention, contention.
Burning to create, not to ablate.
Latticework today, marquetry tomorrow.
No imagination? Execrable display!
Wanton squandering, mind's potential.

Dichotomy

Yea though I walk through the valley of darkness,
The pendulum-swings light my way.
The growing light of hopelessness,
Illuminates my every day.

Speak Up

Go tell it on the mountain,
Or where ever your voice can be heard;
From the cloud forest of Costa Rica,
Convey your mind's word.

It is not in a vain attempt
To vocalize your thoughts,
But merely a narrative
Of fairness, you've been taught.

Listen to others,
As they should listen to you.
Maintain a mental equilibrium,
In what you espouse, and do.

Haunts

I've got shadows all around me
And then more upon the wall;
But I stand alone,
Stooped, not tall.

Shadows can be heavy,
A burden to try and carry.
You're not left in peace,
Unable to linger and tarry.

The light is out.
They still seem to be there.
And all the contemplation,
Still leads you to despair.

Some days, more vague.
Others, like a swarm
That may descend upon you,
And leave you bent and torn.

What egregious sins
Could one have committed
To have a life of torment,
From errors not omitted?

Is it right
To wake,
And think
Life's a mistake?

Conversation with Self

Sane? What a shame
That people can't walk in the rain,
Baring their minds to the winds of pain,
By whatever whim.

Who's to tell us what to do,
The masses, which are me and you,
Or some dark secret hidden in a tome,
Lying on the desk of some disingenuous gnome?

We are as we see ourselves,
Not a case history for shelves,
But unique for others to ponder,
While in our brains we wander.

From the past to today,
Memories go and others stay.
Anxiety builds, won't go away;
Until relief is on the way.

But from what source,
What the course?
Why the torment?
For cerebral firmament?

To get us to the end
Of what we started at birth?
A trip of joy
Down a rocky road?

Peaks and valleys,
Whatever goes.
It's given!
The spirit knows.

What's to stem the tide?
A glance, a thought, a chide,
To reverse abject depression?
A fragrance or meaningful possession?

And are we in command?
If only we could be.
Look into my eyes,
It's me you see.

I am here in my mind.
Listen to the screams.
The ups and down
The rounds and rounds.

In the end there's bliss,
But no time to reminisce.
So, let me do now
What I can't do tomorrow.

Take these demons,
Large and small.
Hide them!
Down a limitless hall.

Please let me steer clear
Of what causes fear.
Let me love, let me live,
Let me sing and let me give.

To myself and to you,
Joy the whole day through.
For if you're happy, then so should be I,
But look at me through my eye.

The truth, evasive, not a chance.
No conveyance through sidewise glance.
A conniving prevaricator,
The master of nothing.

Why can't I have that inner peace?
That all else seem to grasp,
Except for those that think obtusely?
Dejection, depression, what's the use?

Each day, one revolution.
Darwinian --- evolution!
As black is to light,
Then from darkness, to bright!

Dark Hole

I look at that dark hole,
The black tunnel to finality,
The muzzle.
A simple finger flex -
Bang!
It's over.

No time for would-a-could-a-should-a.
Over!
Darkness!
Freedom!

Self-justification

Some need opulence,
Some need pomposity,
Some flamboyance,
Some grandiosity.

Some need extravagance,
Some ostentation,
Some pretention,
Some glorification.

How fragile is thy inner self,
How brittle the confidence
That external observation
Will suffice your requirements.

Surely your laurels,
Whatever they may be,
Are enough to assuage
Your anxiety.

All that effort,
And overt pretention,
Just a fictitious façade.
Why not rely on convention!

Stigma

Is there a stigma in your eye,
Something that you saw,
That you had to try?

An embarrassment gone by,
Yet still exacerbating
Your demeanor … that just won't die.

You ask yourself, why?
Harangued by the unresolvable,
Of what? Loose ends to tie?

Mental maelstrom nigh!
Guilt, an irreparable crease;
Penance gone awry.

State of Self (age 85)

My systems creak and a groan,
Old house in the wintertime,
Shrinkage and decay,
No one home.

Tiny little feet
No longer patter.
Gone with the last crumbs,
Youthful visions no longer matter.

Cling to hope,
Specter of horizons darkening.
Trepidations of early demise,
Exogenous causation, downward slope.

A possible reprieve?
Only if divinely initiated,
But how much time?
Glimmers, only to deceive!

Each day
A new turning,
A restless twenty-four.
The morrow, it may.

Perturbations and anxiety,
Valueless!
Memories depleted,
Exhaustive for piety.

The rotations stare!
No stopping!
Adjust if possible,
Does anyone care?

Four score and five
I have bounced and rolled.
My life seems vacant though.
Virtues of others, I have extolled

Did I symbiotically live
In a contributing sort of way,
Or was I parasitic
And only took, instead give?

Was my love a whim
like a mature dandelion,
To dissolve in a breeze
And blow before the wind?

Retrospection!
A dangerous consideration,
An adventure into an abyss,
Unhealthy reflection.

What laurels to rest on?
Nary a few!
They make no difference
Between me and you.

What impetus to keep up the guile,
To deceive one's self,
Feign happiness,
And keep a smile?

Not a lot!

Sunset Thoughts

My shadow is detached.
What does that portend?
Along the pathway,
the heads are bowed,
A premonition of the end?

It used to be behind me
At the beginning of the day.
As the day grew longer,
It circled me slowly,
towards evening, on its way.

Now I can't catch up!
My shadow is out of sight!

Disquietude

What internal evil engenders my disingenuousness?
Why the on-rush of traducements?
I gather incriminating evidence,
That just might lead me to my life.

Life, but a pasquinade,
A fallacious expression
Of affluence and influence.
Inheritance a stultification!

A travesty in incentivization!
An incoherent assemblage of failed endeavors,
Euphonic or cacophonic,
Little resolution.

No desire to live longer
Than I have tolerance for.
A most mercurial emotion,
Ripe for scarification.

I only know who I am
When I am someone else.
Left to espouse my esoterica,
With the hear-after!

The grand exit,
Natural or committed.
That is the question,
Now submitted.

Why Bother

Why bother to say anything,
When it will always be negated?
Why bother to start a conversation,
When it always gets abated?

Why even try to engage in pleasantries,
When you are met with argumentation?
Why not just pass the time
In retrospective silence ... constructive ideation?

Always something better,
Always another approach.
Is anything ever acceptable?
Enhanced timidity to encroach.

A solo existence could be more meaningful,
Harmony and solace without perplexions.
A whole day could be spent,
without guilty reflections.

But during those few moments of utter tranquility
you know that your love transcends the negativity.
You're destined until death do you part,
Moments to be taken in objectivity

Talking To:

While your soul soars
Through halls of levity,
Mine stagnates
In depressive brevity.

While your vision
Is fogless in clarity,
Mine struggles
Thru dimming disparity.

Then Live!
Incentivization?
Where?
Because you're a biological creation and it is innate.

You can't fight fact,
Consider the positive,
Dump the trite,
Don't be a negetivite.

All five senses
Relatively intact,
Cerebrations,
An abundance thereof.

Climb out of that morass
Of mental ineptitude!
Except the inequities
Of your past and future.

What, you think you're alone!
You're in the league by yourself?
Your hubris is blinding you.
Shed ideation of inevitable nemesis!

Carpe Diem

Too soon the hands of time
Erode our ability to respond
To the natural vicissitudes,
That might now escape our vigilance.

Too soon memories fade,
Eluding reconstruction.
Reminders of what's gone before,
Cascade like autumn leaves from the mind.

Meaningful moments must be spent
Remembering life as past presented;
For our benefit and to remind
Those to come, that life's unique.

Years, days, hours,
Limited by celestial turning,
Mandate response to soul felt yearnings.
Now! Do it now!

Live, love, touch and feel
Your heart and body's screaming urges,
Lest time runs out,
And leaves those lost.

Lost to your life!
Lost to memories!
Lost forever!
Never to be consummated.

Exigencies for the epistler,
Who tries to surmise your thoughts;
Vain attempts to understand
What moved our minds while here,
-- and now gone.

Willingness

Are you willing to accept a no-tomorrow,
And realize that inevitability is nearby?
Perhaps you should endeavor
A stochastic chaos analysis of the Butterfly Effect
On deterministic nonlinear systems.

Does the tail wag the dog or the dog wag the tail?
Did infantile episodes manifest into adult psychoses?
Did a missed breast-feed be the genesis of a foodie …
To create a diabetic and abject neuroses?

Is it just the world we live in, and "So be it!"?
Well, it's certainly ponderable.
But really worth it?

My Life

Did I envision my life to end like this,
a vision through an impenetrable fog,
an existence devoid of meaning, enthusiasm, joy, a raison d'être, and
occasional bliss
Am I to pretend I am whom I am not, a gregarious, extroverted
reasoning individual?
My life was, is now and forever will be, a contradiction.
Where the lust for love, gone now except for backward glances
at what once, was.
A continuum of depressions occasionally interrupted by
fragmentary moments of joy.

A sought-after evasive epiphany to open the door and find a light,
An illumination of my encroaching horizons that would bear an aura
of happiness and contentment.
Is it really worthwhile?
So much for others to gain by my demise,
Except for one, the only one,
That keeps me alive.
But why?

Mindfulness

From the depths of obscurity
To the apex of illumination,
From the doldrums of stagnation
To the zenith of fascination.

So rests the range
Of the human mind,
Only aware to the innermost self
For cognition.

Suffice it to say
That others can only guess
About the veracity
Of your reality.

Tired

I am tired of people trying to orchestrate my life.
I am tired of people trying to eliminate my perception of strife.
I am tired of my whetting the knife.
I am tired.

Why continue this charade?
Why continue this fruitless crusade?
Why continue in someone else's shade?
Why continue?

Why be a sycophant to those you don't respect?
Why be a toady to those who are mentally inept?
Why be obsequious to those you'd like to forget?
Why?

February 13th

So many things to do,
So many places to see;
So many of my loved ones to tell
That they mean so much to me.

The Reaper winks a beckoning call.
Alas! A call I must try and resist.
Let me spend my time with my Mary
And tell Him to cease and desist.

But my chest races at night,
My torso reacts with frightening pain.
I function not as well,
Strength ebbs, loss of aim.

I must hide how I feel
Until a more convenient time.
I tremble with dread,
Yet my life has been sublime.

Even my memory fades,
Yester lore escapes me now,
Except for the long-gone minutia.
The furrows increase on my brow.

If the slide is ahead
And there is no turning back,
Let the world know,
That I have loved without slack.

I have been a gentle man,
A caring, compassionate, good mate.
There's some who doubt,
But that is their mistake.

To live with and be consumed by.
I cannot reach those who don't understand,
Nor should I have tried
For they will sport their mental contraband.

Well, ramble on, I must not,
For time is fleeting and it's rest I need.
My life, should it end abruptly,
Was one filled with love, indeed.

Darkness

Darkness will prevail
At the end of your trail,
With scant little to make it bright.

So, quest thee not
For else to be sought,
It's a life you've created.

Through mazes of miscalculations
And avoidable consternations,
You've stumbled in an erring path.

Your feats not memorable,
Little commendable.
A footprint you will not leave.

Accept your destiny
With a modicum of dignity.
Exit like a man!

One More Time

How many is just one more?
A finite number or time-dependent?
A quantity you want to explore,
Or hang it up and say, "No more!"

Is our life-moment governed,
To be daily warped by the situational,
Or ours to mandate singularly
By individualistic ideation – latitudinal?

Or maybe just say, "f#&k it"!
Leave others to their irritational shouts.
Cash it in, say adios,
Accept defeat ... bow out!

Chapter IV

SHORTS and LIMERICKS

Preamble

No deep philosophical meaning, just a thought or two. Laugh with me or at me … makes little difference, 'cause I have fun.

Thank you to all that can enjoy a little ribaldry and accept jocularity. And to those who are blessed with a degree of acerbity.

"feel ye and thou shall understand"

Heritage

He responded, predominantly atavistic.
When asked his life's characteristic,
If the truth be told
His ancestors were bold,
His destiny, surly hedonistic.

Quest

With research heuristic
And a mindset, sophistic,
He sought in vain
For a singular name,
So adopted a philosophy, pluralistic.

Genesis

Adam: "Now that God's work is done,
"This life should be fun."
Seeking to sate,
Said let's procreate
And that's the way man was begun.

Eve: "Your idea is fine
If not too sublime,
But there seems to be no hurry,
So not to worry.
Nine months will be the time".

Priorities

There was a mathematician named Julian
Whose world appeared cerulean.
When asked his way,
He was heard to say,
I organize my life Boolean.

Guidance

Aimless like a homing pigeon,
Direction, barely a smidgeon.
When faced with grief,
There seemed no relief,
Until he got his religion.

Embarrassment

Disgrace?
Is not always losing face.
In the final analysis
Don't succumb to paralysis,
Examine what took place.

Effort

Some say there's no gain
Unless you have pain.
But to that I say
That notion can't stay,
It's not wholesome in the main.

Arrogance

A superior attitude
And self-perceived beatitude
Does not make you more
Than the fellow next door.
You don't have that latitude.

Bragging

Pseudo-intellectuality,
Not a practicality.
Because your revelations
May need recreations,
And thus, have to face reality.

Society

People come and people go
And people make a splash you know,
It's not how much you spend,
Or how you try to pretend.
In the end, it's about how you grow.

Friends In Need

You think money makes friends?
Be careful what society sends.
Its no joke
When you go broke,
And have no place to make amends.

Climbers

Those who aspire
To socially climb higher,
They may have their day
In some sort of way,
But of them, others will tire.

Evil Doer

He who creates the cuckold
Is a miscreant creature, bold.
Though he dwells with satisfaction,
His life exudes putrefaction
And of his deeds, the world should be told.

"Kiss" (Keep it simple, stupid)

One who is overly pedantic,
To his avocation, semantic,
But try as he might
To think he is right,
He'll never be a romantic.

Table Manners

Whether hypereructatus
Or chronic flatulatus,
The matron was heard to state
To her drunken dining-mate,
From this table there'll be a hiatus.

Self-Control

Give the shopper an inch and they want more.
They salivate in every store.
Try as you might,
They want everything in sight,
No matter how you implore.

Tread Lightly

To walk on thin ice
Is really not nice.
It may result in resentment
And deprive one of contentment.
That would be my advice.

Goals

Rise to the highest level you can.
Aspire to be a man.
For to settle for less
Will bring on stress
And make for an "also-ran."

Preoccupation

The poet, may a pedant be,
Or flit around like a flea.
His work when done,
He feels he's just begun,
And resorts to rhyme instead of thee.

Convictions

Those that create
Oft make the same mistake.
They ask others
Just what are their druthers,
Instead of creating what they like to make.

The Snottier Side

The driving world slides on snot.
Mercedes, Beamer and Lexus owners think they have a lot.
They oft times perceive themselves at the top of the heap,
More socially acceptable than driving a Jeep.

But then there're the Bentleys, Lamborghinis and Ferraris.
Their mere presence makes the others – sorry.
The Rolls roll on the scene,
Their drivers are the only ones serene.

Self-assurance

A word to the wise,
Let there be no compromise.
Stick to your convictions,
Avoid derelictions,
And above all others, rise.

Money Hole

To own a boat
Is like having a goat,
It's appetite never to sate.
An insatiable beast, to say the least,
Repairs, never to wait.

Marital Morality

For every do'or, there's a do'ee
As complicated as that may be.
It's senseless to blame just one
Under this heavenly sun.
The problem is twofold, you see.

Inferiority

Don't assume someone is better than you,
Just because they look you through.
Let them take a chance
And wear your pants.
See just how well they do.

Addle Headed

You could tell by the viscosity
There wasn't cerebral porosity.
Not that it makes any difference,
But there's certainly the inference
That he is a bit of a curiosity.

People

From others, have no expectations.
There'll be few trials and tribulations.
You won't be sad
If things get bad.
If good, extol congratulations.

Political Animosities

Your search for surcease
Will only increase
Your continued vexation.
The problem persists
When the world insists
On hiding any cessation.

Family

There are special relations
That call for libations.
And then there are others
Whose fathers and mothers,
Deny that they are their creations.

Overly Analytical

"Regression analysis
May cause paralysis,"
The teacher was heard to say.
The confusion may go away,
But not without renal dialysis.

Religiosity

I thought you knew
That sitting in a pew
Would not increase your speed
To heaven indeed,
Nor with sanctity, you imbue.

Your ascendancy should be ascribed
To something inside
And not an exhibition
Of sobriety and no imbibition,
But rather what you've decried.

So your soul will rest
Not on haste but the best
Of what your character will unveil.
It may well be a test
Of what your travails will entail.

Let-down

You go to the store for something terrific
And need assistance specific.
But advice received is not timely,
Yet given sublimely.
It turns out pretty horrific.

Word Play

So, you schlepped like a baby.
Don't you think maybe,
That for the sake of pride,
You should soon decide
And like a man, someday be?

Cooking

The amateur chef is in need
Of a glass of wine indeed.
It adds to his confidence
To cook without consequence
And enhance his endeavor to succeed.

Clothing

Underwear is for hair and such
And other things not to touch.
But lest it seem crude,
I'd rather go nude,
And not have to care so much.

Women

Suspicious, malicious, pique,
All in the feminine mystique.
Is it any wonder
That we are torn asunder,
And that we call their gender unique?

Mystery

Ladies remain a mystery to me.
To the depth of their soul, you'll never see.
But I guess it's supposed to be that way,
Listening to what our mothers had to say
Whilst they bounced us on their knee.

Mystique

Mystique is the feminine gender,
Something that husbands should remember.
If their memories should fail,
Then let good sense prevail;
And let them realize what gender is the mender.

And should the wives not be aware
That their husbands may act like a bear;
Let them soon realize
And not be taken by surprise
That in love, anything is fair.

Red Neck Socialite

I got a real big diamond ring,
A beautiful convertible Jag,
A million-dollar outfit,
And a Wal-Mart garment bag.

I'm a red neck socialite.
Nothing bothers me,
A Styrofoam cup of warm Cold Duck
Or a high-class cup of tea.

Nosey Ones

For people who delve into other people's lives,
It should be no surprise
That the gossip they find,
Doesn't benefit their mind,
And does not make them wise.

Less is More

There was a lady of inestimable esteem,
Who lest she be taken for more than she did mean,
Couched her phraseology
To concur with her ideology,
That less is more, it would seem.

Few Words

A lady, who relished to be ravished in bed,
Was probed for thoughts in her head.
When queried quite distinctly,
She uttered quite succinctly,
"Copies" was all she said.

Stats

There once was a statistician
Who aspired to be a magician.
Try as he might,
He was not too bright
And succumbed to his own ambition.

Not Relevant

There once was a statistician
Who thought he was a magician.
He must have been dreaming while in bed,
'Cause what he thought was exact,
Was not really fact,
Professional Reviews he should have read.

More Stats

There was a statistician
Who thought himself a logician.
He didn't get the point
That for him to self-anoint,
Was hardly an act of contrition.

More Stats 2

Numerical deceivers
To sway non-believers.
Statistics pave the way
For others to say
That they enable wordy weavers.

MD Escapism

My specialty is quite defining.
If you have problems that need refining,
I would suggest you see
Someone other than me,
'Cause your malady escapes my designing.

Ants

It was the biologist's observation,
With astute characterization
That the Robin by chance,
Has ants in his pants,
A degree of sublime formication.

Auto Arrogance

Four cars to the corner did hesitate;
The Rolls went first
With an energy burst,
The Mercedes was next
Leaving the Beemer perplexed.
The Ford, he had to wait.

Sing a Song

It is oft said that beneath the moon
Only fools will choose to croon.
And I would implore,
To the neighbor next door,
That you consider changing your tune.

Fads

If it's a diet
Try it.
If you want to get small
Don't eat at all.
And with food, just don't buy it.

Commerce

When you have something that others might want,
You may have adequate reason to taunt.
If they want it free,
You simply just flee,
And entice them with an occasional vaunt.

If it is naturally commercial
There's no need for rehearsal.
You can achieve perfection
Over another's objection
And leave them hopelessly penurial.

Eco 101

Why does it get so intense
When you talk about dollars and cents?
It's impossible to be luxurious
When you must be penurious
And run into a problem so dense.

Eco 102

Why is there no romance
When you talk about finance?
Unanimity of opinion?
Not in your dominion.
Parity, not a chance.

Living Rationale

Have you ever thought about the male animal,
And what he was put on earth to do?
Why procreate the species,
And do unto others before they do unto you.

Depression

Have you ever wanted to write a song
And realized the words were all wrong?
No way for gaiety and words to merge.
You'd do better with a dirge.
Your mood is abysmal,
Your outlook dismal,

America

There was a fine country, America
With people from Shanghai to Billerica.
A true melting pot there,
With inventions everywhere,
From the profound to just esoterica.

Maturity

It takes many years to achieve maturity,
But still with questionable security.
With children and such,
The entry fee's too much,
To run in a human futurity.

Your Cheek

Life is turning the other cheek.
With your children, its love they should seek.
Why then should they be so mean?
In the face of logicality, it would seem,
That their role should be more meek.

Your Children

How quickly children forget
Who dried them when they were wet,
Who took them fishing, skiing and more,
Who comforted them when they were sore,
Yet they always try for more than they should get.

Parental Wrong?

Where does a parent go wrong in doing all that they can do,
In attending to every need, always something else, always something new?
Why is enough never enough and there always has to be more?
Why is the younger generation never satisfied until they have gnawed your very core?
Is it just because they are adamant about having their cake and eating it too?

Speak Your Piece

Limericize to philosophize.
To others, be thought not wise,
But to hell with them for they know not
What inner pain you've got.
State your feelings under whatever guise.

The Change

What ever happened to your child
Who was so loving and mild?
What changed within their heart,
To rip the parental tie apart?
You used to rapture when they smiled.

Frustration

A quest for independence achieved?
A state of melancholy for a mother bereaved?
Do you think you'll ever know
What will make the relationship grow?
No! You'll never be believed.

You to Me

Nonparametric statistics would agree
That love is a chance phenomenon, can't you see?
A complex random act,
Not quantitative by fact.
It was making order out of chaos that brought you to me.

Arrogance

You are a Rancho resident
And it makes you feel like a president,
But if you should think
Your waste doesn't stink,
Perhaps you should be more hesitant.

Numbers Together

Said a mathematician to his statistician friend,
Numerically, you are the living end.
Said she to he, your numbers I can't ignore
I lust for them and more.
So off they went, the rest of their lives to spend.

Observe

The turtle is no lout,
He knows how to mount.
Lest there be some doubt,
As to ability and clout,
Baby turtles you should count.

Sicily

There was a young lady, Scarlato
Who had a devious ploto
To capture her man,
Which she knew she can
As success is a Sicilian motto.

Etherion

There was a Goddess from Etherion
Who had her beauty quite clearly on.
When to earth she came,
Men's hearts she did maim,
Until captured by her Hyperion.

Mars

There was a young lady from Mars
Who liked to frequent bars.
While in San Lucas,
She bared her tucas,
And caused a lot of Har! Hars!

Poetic Regimen

Fourteen lines a sonnet hath
To curve down a poet's path.
But times more or less are heeded,
And poetic etiquette is little needed.

Domesticity

Hold handle down for a complete flush,
Lest it all come back as disgusting mush.
And I with a plunger, must vigorously attack
To make sure that next time – it doesn't come back.

Unhappy Patient

Inaccurate diagnoses, medical hacks
Bloody surgeons with poorly sterilized packs.
Why take so many trips
Just to go to Scripps,
When the local duck pond has just as many quacks.

Psychiatrist

A shrink
To make you think
You've got erratic
Static
In your attic.

My Lady

My lady said it was permissible,
So I found her neck quite kissable.
One thing led to another
And now our daughters have a brother.
I do find my lady irresistible.

Sagacity

Oh, to be born with unfathomable sagacity,
It would be the ultimate in mendacity.
For to have that sort of desire,
Would anatomically require,
A cranium beyond humanoid capacity.

Vanity

What is there to gain
By being inordinately vain?
The mirror reflects you as you are
Every line, blemish and scar.
Learn to live with it; yourself, remain.

Cooking

To cook by the book
Might cause you to overlook
A delectable tidbit or herb
That others might think absurd.
You'd not know just what you forsook.

Sewing

Said the seamstress to the cook in the kitchen,
"I'm sure you find this really bitchin.
But to be quite frank,
A hem I'd rather yank
And spend the rest of the time, a stitchin'."

Polishing Shoes

To polish shoes,
To some might amuse,
But I think I'd rather
Avoid working up a lather,
Than thus my dignity abuse.

Ironing

To iron is a ridiculous kind of stress,
To de-wrinkle some fancy dress.
Why not buy wrinkle free
And avoid domesticity?
Of the duress, you'd have less.

Drivers

To the solo driver in the car pool lane,
The cop said, "You give me a pain."
So she quickly replied,
"That cannot be denied",
But not to be here, would be insane.

Lack of Curiosity

They only know
What they had been told.
How limited their vision!
If the truth be known,
Then perhaps less derision.

Complainers

Those that always complain,
Should have it inherent in their game,
That their main apprehension,
Is that no one will pay attention.

Determination

Where are you going red ant?
To cross the Sahara, you can't.
Yet trudge you must
Through all that dust,
Because to quit you shan't.

Why

Goodness gracious me oh my!
I sometimes wonder why
We keep on trying to please others,
Until the day we die.

Deception

Deception is the work of angels,
When plighted against the ones they love.
As we male mortals bumble as clueless,
They conjure up --- with blessing from above.

Gentleman's

A gentleman's healthy proclivity
For sexual activity,
May sometimes with age, wane;
But his voyeuristic lust,
Whether for bush or bust,
Seems always to remain the same.

A Woman

A woman wouldn't be a woman
Unless she had the last word.
To think otherwise is blatantly absurd.

So you men beware
Who'd like to dare,
It's insane and utter defeat.

Intellect

There was a lady of intellectuality
Who decided to learn about reality.
So to college she went,
Where most of her time was spent,
Learning about consensuality.

Talk Talk

"All I have to do is talk," said she,
And others will listen to me.
But when she opened her mouth,
Her friends went south,
In a vain attempt to flee.

Maiden's Cry

There was a cry from the maid,
Who said she was really afraid
To lie in the sun
And have some fun;
So said he, "You can get made in the shade."

Mysterious One

In a woman's pique
There's an amazing mystique.
Cross her path
And you incur her wrath.
And never will there be a critique.

Lady in Waiting

There was a lady in waiting
Who really desired a mating,
But try as she might,
He slipped out of sight,
And left her anxiously grating.

To Bed

I really like this bed
And that was not all she said.
When she laid her body down,
There was nary a frown,
As her man, to bed she led.

Control

The emanation was with steam,
Or so it did seam.
T 'was because she was fearful
Of becoming quite tearful
And inappropriately venting her spleen.

Maternal Flaw

They only knew an incorrect decision.
How limited their vision!
What their mother had related,
Was something she created
And the cause of much derision.

Windwalker

A lovely 54' sailing vessel – yawl

Windwalker – An honorable sport
Nere to be a duplicated sort!
She plied the Seven Seas
With strength in her knees.
Dazzling, she would slide into port.

Wise! Quietly she would sail
Leaving envy off her rail.
Those to observe,
They lacked the verve,
To venture they would fail.

Me, Myself and I

Me myself and I,
I tried not to cry
As I sat there all alone
In my floating home.

Too Late

Raise your hands above your head,
Sing a song for the living and the dead.
Tell them how you love them so.
For some it's too late,
They had to go.

Boats

There was a man who aspired for a yacht.
Now in some circles that's a lot.
No matter what people had to say,
He went ahead a spent all his pay.
Now he wishes that he had not!

The Party

The party's over
But who in the Hell attended?
It is only in retrospect
That the activities shall be amended.

It was fun while it lasted.
Some I just can't remember.
There were ups and downs
And rounds and rounds
And just a few up-ended.

But all in all
Not a bad blast.
All things considered
Too bad it couldn't last.

Barista Louisa

Pleasa, pleasa, Barista
Won't you giva to me,
An iced, non-fat, latte,
That'sa what I want, you see.

And if I don't say Pleasa,
In the right way,
Then per piacere, por favor
And si vous plait.

And when you give it to me,
If I no thank you as you wan me to,
Then mange tak, dankeschön,
And merci beaucoup.

Now I hava no more money
I can no buy from you,
So arn you glad now,
This song isa finally through?

Seventies

I once knew a man who was seventy-two
And most everything he said was true,
But on the calendar he had the wrong page
And didn't really know his age,
For there was nothing this man wouldn't do.

Patriotic Old Driller

My well's been plugged
And my pump's been takin' out,
But what the hell,
That's what age is all about.

Turn the page,
Read another line.
Ain't so bad,
I really feel fine.

Women still like me.
Don't have to get up at night.
I like what I feel
And I feel what is right.

No paternal worries!
Arriving early is rare.
God Bless America!
My casing is still there.

So drill as I may
And drill as I might,
I'll drill everything
That I see in my sight.

Oh say does that banner still wave
Ore the wellheads of the free,
And the groans
Of the brave.

More Stats

There was a statistician
Who thought he was a magician
In deceiving the public so deftly.
But he was hardly aware
That his arrogant air
Was making him calculate ineptly.

Gobble-Gobble

Turkeys walk
And Turkeys talk
And some are shot you know.
But wild turkey meat is not tender,
Regardless of their gender.
So leave them in the wild to grow!

Ace Hardware

A towering pillar of startling erudition
Began my day with a product rendition.
Nothing related to what I wanted,
His incomprehension freely flaunted,
So I retreated in humble submission.

Rocky Springtime

An inch or two on the ground and piling high,
Why by noon, it may be up to the sky.
But that's really great,
All the locals state,
But on the third of May, WHY?

Weatherman

The local meteorologist
Ought to see a psychologist
To figure out his objective;
To try and lie,
Or try to tell why,
His forecasts are not more subjective.

Frustration Avoidance

If perturbed by a mono-synaptic misfiring,
Then avoid all situations requiring
An answer coherent
That might be adherent
To something logically desiring.

Boar's Butt
A restaurant somewhere in Colorado

"Boar's Butt"
Or a decent Prime Cut,
The quality is simply not there.

I'll pay for a good meal.
I'm not trying to steal.
Just please tell me where!

Over-rated

The restaurant may pretend
There're tops, they contend.
But try for service
Amongst a staff too nervous,
It's not worth what you have to spend.

Carmel

The Golden flecks upon the sea
Singing softly to me.
Come, come!
I am the setting sun.

Job-site flirtation

Said he, "Let me see your knees."
Said she, "Just a little tease!"
Emotions they couldn't deny
Led to her post-coital cry,
"Copies if you please."

Senorita Superiority

Said a sweet Hispanic lass,
"I see you covet my ass.
No es mi problema,
Es su dilemma.
It's obvious you have no class."

Admonishment

Exacerbations, exasperations, aggravations,
Vexations, irritations,
Nothing but stressful!
Time well spent
Should lead to something more restful.

Sergeant Cook

Not a drop, yust a pinch,
Do it my vay, I don't give an inch.
Zere vill be a soupçon, not a splash,
And vit de spice - yust a dash.

Undt der pots vill be clean,
Or I get exceptionally mean.
Undt here you put ze rag,
No, you fool …. in ze bag.

Undt ve only use vot is lean,
Ya! Yust a little gream.
Alvays a bit of zest,
I know vot vould be best.

You may haf maybe your own tought,
But remember, it is me you brought.
So in ze end you vill do it my vay,
For zat is vot I say!

Expectancy

There is a younger population
Anticipating adulation.
And even if not earned,
They should not be spurned;
Why it's a natural expectation.

A Woman

A woman's divine complexity,
Uniqueness ethereal -
A man's perplexity,
And a mystique surreal.

The Beckoning Way

Lead on
Or let me go first,
For exploration
I do thirst.

Travel by day?
I'd rather not by night.
You can't see more
Than when it is light.

Color Your World

A Fall endeavor,
Color your world
With thoughts chromatic.
A time for introspection
And a fragrant aromatic.

I Am

Why should I take time for people
Who don't take time for me?
A quirk of my character, don't you see?
No need to reason or rhyme
With those who might take up my time.
I am who I am, and just who I want to be.

The Therapist

The master of rejuvenescence!
She claims a simple manipulation,
But perfection is surely the essence
Of sublime rejuvenation.

BPPV

Those with otoliths, errant,
Their discomfort is very apparent.
They're dizzy when they rise,
Which is no surprise,
And their behavior becomes quite aberrant.

Booze and Wine

Lemons and limes,
Booze and Wine,
That's all a good bar needs.
Oh wait! That's not enough.
You have to have people
Who like the stuff.

Bill Fish

Behold the tragic pelagic!
He's as forlorn as it would seem.
He travels with might
All day and all night
Just to catch a lesser piscine.

Life

The longer we live
The shorter our life!
A seeming dichotomy,
Perplexities rife!

Lazy

Procrastination is the seat for lethargy
Or does the latter come first?
Will the morn even evolve,
Without the verve for thirst?

Autumn

Summer days close.
Warm shadows to a deep repose,
Colors come out of hiding,
To natures call – abiding!

Whispers

Such words caress my very being -
It was not a dream,
But rather an angel
Enriching my life;
Now flown to a new horizon.

Expectations

To be spoiled is to expect.
Tis a feeling that's not correct.
To others, full of expectations,-
They're worthy of excoriations!
An assumed birthright? –
With reality, a disconnect!

Materialism

Are you incarcerated by materialism?
Is wishful thinking – a "No"!
Do you feel your life style is inhibited?
Then you may have to let it go!

A change may be in order
To a more suitable place.
Your years may pass you by,
If you don't alter your pace.

Hurry

Do you relish with gusto,
Or do you make every tidbit last?
Is it better to enjoy now,
Or dwindle out till the present is past?

Morality

It is not a question of morality
It is just worldly reality.
For every do-or, there is a do-ee.
Blatantly obvious, can't you see?
Strictly a matter of consensually!

Epicurean

Oh, to be in a home as a gourmand
Where variety was accepted de rigueur.
It would be like waving a magic wand,
Not to have to cook for just her.

In Flagranti

Life a lie and what then?
Not an option to start again.
The trail you started,
Twisted, unfinished, wantonly abandoned,
Disrespected - gifts untold.
What engendered that weakness of gene?
In the face of a cornucopia of opportunities,
Decisions obscene.

Change

Why is that we relish
What we can embellish
And not be satisfied with the status quo?
Is it our own reflection
Of our own complexion,
And a fear of the after-glow?

Quit Dreamin'

I don't know what tomorrow brings,
Sorrow, or what the angels sing.
Mine is not to question why,
But to accept that dreams don't fly.

Last Dish

Actuality in reality it does not exist.
It is only our longings that continually persist.
The inevitable acceptance of fate
Must be the last dish upon our plate.

Negativity

There was one who had the proclivity
For unbounded negativity.
Though really not sound,
There seemed to be a ground
For the Church's liceity.

Post Prandial "Prime Ten"
Parking lot, fancy restaurant

"Mercedes, "500", Aubergine,"
The call to the Valet for his machine.
My turn next,
And lest the Valet be perplexed,
I clearly gave a shout
To eliminate any doubt,
"Dodge, Rental, Enterprise".

Whispering, "Try that one for size."

A social atrocity
To balance pomposity.
As I departed, a fiver I did tip.
"Thank you," the reply.
"The other guy's a gyp."
"You're more fun,
The other guy gave me a one."

Long Gone Doggie Blues

Have you seen your doggie up in heaven?
Have you seen your Bow-Wow in the sky?
Have you seen your Poochie-Pie riding on a rainbow?
Did you get a chance to tell your doggie Bye Bye?

Remember the rabbits he used to chase,
And just how he licked you in the face?
Well it's time to realize you can't look him in the eyes,
And another has just got to take his place.
I got The Long-Gone Doggie Blues!

Remodel Blues

Can't find my clothes,
'Cause there in the kitchen.
The shovels are in my closet,
And that's really bitchin'.

There goes the bathroom and soon the garage.
Got no place to eat.
Hole in the roof lets me see the moon.
Got no place to put my feet.

The toilet's where it belongs,
But there's no toilet paper.
Five more months,
Of this re-model caper.

I've got the re-model blues.
Can't find my shoes.
The freezer's unplugged
And the disposal's full of screws.

Turned to find the front door,
But the front door wasn't there.
Just part of a cement mixer,
Putting cement everywhere.

No more circuits working,
They've all been blown.
Power tools smoking,
No more money in the loan.

In for a penny, in for a pound,
I've got the re-model blues.
Can't stop it now,
What do I have to lose?

My sanity is all
And maybe my wife.
Bit off more my than I could chew,
No more remodel in my life.

"Short job," contractor said.
My life is at the bottom of the well.
Now I wish he were dead.
Used to be heaven, now I'm in hell.

I've got the remodel blues!

Time & Rhyme

There was a time sublime
When things didn't rhyme,
But they are past.
Serenity doesn't last,
Now poetry is mine.

SENTITO et INTELLEGITO

www.ingramcontent.com/pod-product-compliance
Lightning Source LLC
Chambersburg PA
CBHW070054030426
42335CB00016B/1885